At Issue

The Ethics of Capital Punishment

Christine Watkins, Book Editor

GREENHAVEN PRESS
A part of Gale, Cengage Learning

GALE
CENGAGE Learning

Detroit • New York • San Francisco • New Haven, Conn • Waterville, Maine • London

GALE
CENGAGE Learning™

Christine Nasso, *Publisher*
Elizabeth Des Chenes, *Managing Editor*

© 2011 Greenhaven Press, a part of Gale, Cengage Learning.

Gale and Greenhaven Press are registered trademarks used herein under license.

For more information, contact:
Greenhaven Press
27500 Drake Rd.
Farmington Hills, MI 48331-3535
Or you can visit our Internet site at gale.cengage.com

For product information and technology assistance, contact us at

Gale Customer Support, 1-800-877-4253
For permission to use material from this text or product, submit all requests online at
www.cengage.com/permissions

Further permissions questions can be emailed to permissionrequest@cengage.com

Articles in Greenhaven Press anthologies are often edited for length to meet page requirements. In addition, original titles of these works are changed to clearly present the main thesis and to explicitly indicate the author's opinion. Every effort is made to ensure that Greenhaven Press accurately reflects the original intent of the authors. Every effort has been made to trace the owners of copyrighted material.

Cover Image copyright © Images.com/Corbis.

LIBRARY OF CONGRESS CATALOGING-IN-PUBLICATION DATA

The ethics of capital punishment / Christine Watkins, book editor.
    p. cm. -- (At issue)
Includes bibliographical references and index.
ISBN 978-0-7377-5171-0 (hardcover) -- ISBN 978-0-7377-5172-7 (pbk.)
1. Capital punishment--Moral and ethical aspects--United States--Juvenile literature. I. Watkins, Christine, 1951-
HV8699.U5E842 2011
172'.2--dc22
                                     2010036737

Contents

Introduction

On February 17, 2004, the state of Texas executed Cameron Todd Willingham by lethal injection for intentionally setting his house on fire in 1991, killing his two-year-old daughter and one-year-old twin daughters. Prior to the execution, Dr. Gerald Hurst, a highly esteemed scientist and fire investigator, examined the evidence in the case against Willingham and concluded that the fire had actually been accidental, probably the result of a malfunctioning space heater or faulty wiring. Hurst found no evidence to support arson charges and wrote a report to that effect in an attempt to stay Willingham's execution. But no one at the Board of Pardons and Paroles or the Texas governor's office paid any attention, and Willingham was executed on schedule. After the execution, three more independent investigations of the Willingham case—in 2004, 2006, and 2007—concluded that there was no scientific basis for claiming Willingham had intentionally set the fire. Before he was put to death, Willingham told the Associated Press, "The most distressing thing is the state of Texas will kill an innocent man and doesn't care they're making a mistake."

Such a case represents a horrifying scenario for opponents of capital punishment because killing an innocent person is irrevocable, leaving no room for atonement or to make amends. Stuart Banner wrote in his 2002 book *The Death Penalty*, "The prospect of killing an innocent person seemed to be the one thing that could cause people to rethink their support for capital punishment." But is that true? Would executing a clearly innocent person lead opponents and supporters of capital punishment to finally reach some sort of agreement regarding the issue? Not exactly.

In 2009, Gallup's annual Crime Survey indicated that 65 percent of Americans support capital punishment for the crime of murder. The Gallup poll also found that 59 percent of Americans believe that within the last five years "a person has been executed under the death penalty who was, in fact, innocent of the crime he or she was charged with." Furthermore, of those Americans who believe an innocent person has been executed, 57 percent still support the death penalty. And while opponents of the death penalty cite the fact that there have been 254 post-conviction DNA exonerations in the United States as proof of the criminal justice system's fallibility, many death penalty supporters fire back that the long process of appeals and the advent of DNA testing have resulted in capital punishment becoming a more reliable and mistake-proof punishment than ever before. Supreme Court Justice Antonin Scalia defended this conviction in his opinion regarding a 2006 Kansas death penalty case: "The dissent makes much of the new-found capacity of DNA testing to establish innocence. But in every case of an executed defendant of which I am aware, that technology has confirmed guilt." Frank Jung, a Missouri assistant attorney general, discounted DNA testing even further by declaring in 2003 before the Missouri Supreme Court that even when DNA evidence reveals a wrongful conviction, the condemned inmate should be executed anyway. Billy Wayne Sinclair and Jodie Sinclair explained in their book *Capital Punishment: An Indictment by a Death-Row Survivor*, "Jung is part of a league of prosecutors who feel that claims of innocence should not be entertained by the courts after the trial and appeal in a criminal case. They believe that the criminal justice system's interest in the 'finality of conviction' is more important than saving an innocent man from death."

On the other hand, many Americans—including supporters of the death penalty—are horrified at the thought of executing an innocent person. A good example is George Ryan, a longtime advocate of capital punishment and the governor of the state of Illinois from 1999 until January 2003. In 2000, after thirteen people on death row were exonerated through

DNA evidence, Ryan suspended the death penalty in his state, declaring that he could no longer support a system that has "come so close to the ultimate nightmare—the state's taking of innocent life." Ryan went on to say, "There is a flaw in the system, without question, and it needs to be studied."

In fact, the Innocence Project, an organization that works to exonerate the wrongfully convicted, does just that—studies the systemic defects in the US criminal justice system. According to the Innocence Project, mistaken eyewitness identification was a factor in 75 percent of post-conviction DNA exonerations in the United States; false confessions and incriminating statements led to wrongful convictions in approximately 25 percent of cases; and unreliable informant testimony contributed to 19 percent of wrongful convictions. "And it is perfectly clear to all who are observant that those with more money and better lawyers have a much better chance of being exonerated of a crime than those who have neither, whether the exoneration is just or unjust," wrote biblical scholar and author Ben Witherington on his January 15, 2007, blog. "Statistics suggest," Witherington wrote, "that many, many cases exist of persons on death row who are not there because they are guilty of the crime. What they are guilty of is having bad legal representation, or even worse they are guilty of being poor or mentally incompetent to defend themselves."

The death penalty will continue to be one of the most passionately debated issues in the United States, and perhaps throughout the entire world. The authors in *At Issue: The Ethics of Capital Punishment* discuss other legal, moral, and practical aspects of this complex issue.

1

The Death Penalty Violates the Constitution of the United States

Justice John Paul Stevens

Nominated by President Gerald Ford, John Paul Stevens served as an Associate Justice of the Supreme Court of the United States from 1975 until he retired in 2010.

In the United States, the primary justification for imposing the death penalty is retribution, in which the perpetrator receives adequate punishment for the crime committed against the victim. The Eighth Amendment to the U.S. Constitution, however, prohibits the use of cruel and unusual or excessive punishment, and thus protects the wrongdoer from receiving a punishment that is comparable to the suffering inflicted on the victim, in effect negating the possibility of retribution. Furthermore, emotional impact, biased jurors, and discriminatory application of death penalty cases work to create a real risk of wrongful convictions. Therefore, a penalty more severe than imprisonment without the possibility of parole is excessive and violates the Constitution.

Current decisions by state legislatures, by the Congress of the United States, and by this Court to retain the death penalty as a part of our law are the product of habit and inattention rather than an acceptable deliberative process that

Justice John Paul Stevens, "Justice Stevens, Concurring in Judgment, Supreme Court of the United States, No. 07-5439, Ralph Baze and Thomas C. Bowling, Petitioners *v.* John D. Rees, Commissioner, Kentucky Department of Corrections, et al.," www.supreme court.gov, pp. 8–17.

weighs the costs and risks of administering that penalty against its identifiable benefits, and rest in part on a faulty assumption about the retributive force of the death penalty.

Justification for the Death Penalty

In *Gregg v. Georgia* (1976), we explained that unless a criminal sanction serves a legitimate penological function, it constitutes "gratuitous infliction of suffering" in violation of the Eighth Amendment. We then identified three societal purposes for death as a sanction: incapacitation, deterrence, and retribution. In the past three decades, however, each of these rationales has been called into question.

It is the retribution rationale that animates much of the remaining enthusiasm for the death penalty.

While incapacitation may have been a legitimate rationale in 1976, the recent rise in statutes providing for life imprisonment without the possibility of parole demonstrates that incapacitation is neither a necessary nor a sufficient justification for the death penalty. Moreover, a recent poll indicates that support for the death penalty drops significantly when life without the possibility of parole is presented as an alternative option. And the available sociological evidence suggests that juries are less likely to impose the death penalty when life without parole is available as a sentence.

The legitimacy of deterrence as an acceptable justification for the death penalty is also questionable, at best. Despite 30 years of empirical research in the area, there remains no reliable statistical evidence that capital punishment in fact deters potential offenders. In the absence of such evidence, deterrence cannot serve as a sufficient penological justification for this uniquely severe and irrevocable punishment.

We are left, then, with retribution as the primary rationale for imposing the death penalty. And indeed, it is the retribution rationale that animates much of the remaining enthusiasm for the death penalty. As Lord Justice Denning [of England and Wales] argued in 1950, "some crimes are so outrageous that society insists on adequate punishment, because the wrong-doer deserves it, irrespective of whether it is a deterrent or not." Our Eighth Amendment jurisprudence has narrowed the class of offenders eligible for the death penalty to include only those who have committed outrageous crimes defined by specific aggravating factors. It is the cruel treatment of victims that provides the most persuasive arguments for prosecutors seeking the death penalty. A natural response to such heinous crimes is a thirst for vengeance.

The Diminished Capacity of Retribution

At the same time, however, . . . our society has moved away from public and painful retribution towards ever more humane forms of punishment. State-sanctioned killing is therefore becoming more and more anachronistic [out of date]. In an attempt to bring executions in line with our evolving standards of decency, we have adopted increasingly less painful methods of execution, and then declared previous methods barbaric and archaic [primitive]. But by requiring that an execution be relatively painless, we necessarily protect the inmate from enduring any punishment that is comparable to the suffering inflicted on his victim. This trend, while appropriate and required by the Eighth Amendment's prohibition on cruel and unusual punishment, actually undermines the very premise on which public approval of the retribution rationale is based. . . .

Full recognition of the diminishing force of the principal rationales for retaining the death penalty should lead this Court and legislatures to reexamine the question recently [2006] posed by Professor Salinas, a former Texas prosecutor and judge: "Is it time to Kill the Death Penalty?" The time for a dispassionate, impartial comparison of the enormous costs that death penalty litigation imposes on society with the benefits that it produces has surely arrived.

[According to *Furman v. Georgia* (1972)], "[A] penalty may be cruel and unusual because it is excessive and serves no valid legislative purpose." Our cases holding that certain sanctions are "excessive," and therefore prohibited by the Eighth Amendment, have relied heavily on "objective criteria," such as legislative enactments. In our recent decision in *Atkins v. Virginia* (2002), holding that death is an excessive sanction for a mentally retarded defendant, we also relied heavily on opinions written by Justice [Byron Raymond] White holding that the death penalty is an excessive punishment for the crime of raping a 16-year-old woman, *Coker v. Georgia* (1977), and for a murderer who did not intend to kill, *Enmund v. Florida* (1982). In those opinions we acknowledged that "objective evidence, though of great importance, did not 'wholly determine' the controversy, 'for the Constitution contemplates that in the end our own judgment will be brought to bear on the question of the acceptability of the death penalty under the Eighth Amendment.'" . . .

Inadequate Procedures in Death Penalty Cases

Our decisions in 1976 upholding the constitutionality of the death penalty relied heavily on our belief that adequate procedures were in place that would avoid the danger of discriminatory application. In subsequent years a number of our decisions relied on the premise that "death is different" from every other form of punishment to justify rules minimizing the risk of error in capital cases. Ironically, however, more recent cases have endorsed procedures that provide less protections to capital defendants than to ordinary offenders.

Of special concern to me are rules that deprive the defendant of a trial by jurors representing a fair cross section of the community. Litigation involving both challenges for cause and peremptory challenges has persuaded me that the process of obtaining a "death qualified jury" is really a procedure that has the purpose and effect of obtaining a jury that is biased in favor of conviction. The prosecutorial concern that death verdicts would rarely be returned by 12 randomly selected jurors should be viewed as objective evidence supporting the conclusion that the penalty is excessive.

A third significant concern is the risk of discriminatory application of the death penalty.

The Risk of Error and Discrimination

Another serious concern is that the risk of error in capital cases may be greater than in other cases because the facts are often so disturbing that the interest in making sure the crime does not go unpunished may overcome residual doubt concerning the identity of the offender. Our former emphasis on the importance of ensuring that decisions in death cases be adequately supported by reason rather than emotion, has been undercut by more recent decisions placing a thumb on the prosecutor's side of the scales. Thus, in *Kansas v. Marsh* (2006), the Court upheld a state statute that requires imposition of the death penalty when the jury finds that the aggravating and mitigating factors are in equipoise [balance]. And in *Payne v. Tennessee* (1991), the Court overruled earlier cases and held that "victim impact" evidence relating to the personal characteristics of the victim and the emotional impact of the crime on the victim's family is admissible despite the fact that it sheds no light on the question of guilt or innocence or on the moral culpability of the defendant, and thus serves no purpose other than to encourage jurors to make life or death decisions on the basis of emotion rather than reason.

A third significant concern is the risk of discriminatory application of the death penalty. While that risk has been dramatically reduced, the Court has allowed it to continue to play an unacceptable role in capital cases. Thus, in *McCleskey v. Kemp* (1987), the Court upheld a death sentence despite the "strong probability that [the defendant's] sentencing jury . . . was influenced by the fact that [he was] black and his victim was white." . . .

Finally, given the real risk of error in this class of cases, the irrevocable nature of the consequences is of decisive importance to me. Whether or not any innocent defendants have actually been executed, abundant evidence accumulated in recent years has resulted in the exoneration of an unacceptable number of defendants found guilty of capital offenses. The risk of executing innocent defendants can be entirely eliminated by treating any penalty more severe than life imprisonment without the possibility of parole as constitutionally excessive.

In sum, just as Justice White ultimately based his conclusion in *Furman* on his extensive exposure to countless cases for which death is the authorized penalty, I have relied on my own experience in reaching the conclusion that the imposition of the death penalty represents "the pointless and needless extinction of life with only marginal contributions to any discernible social or public purposes. A penalty with such negligible returns to the State [is] patently excessive and cruel and unusual punishment violative of the Eighth Amendment."

2

The Death Penalty Does Not Violate the US Constitution

Justice Antonin Gregory Scalia

Appointed by President Ronald Reagan in 1986, Antonin Gregory Scalia became the Senior Associate Justice of the US Supreme Court in 2010 when Justice John Paul Stevens retired.

The US Constitution specifically allows for the death penalty to be imposed as a criminal sanction, and democratically elected legislatures—not court justices—should decide if and when to use it. Among the justifications for capital punishment are deterrence and retribution. Determining the value of such deterrence and retribution rests not with judicial opinion, but with the experience and wisdom of the American people.

Justice [John Paul] Stevens concludes [his opinion] as follows: "[T]he imposition of the death penalty represents the pointless and needless extinction of life with only marginal contributions to any discernible social or public purposes. A penalty with such negligible returns to the State [is] patently excessive and cruel and unusual punishment violative of the Eighth Amendment."

The Courts Have No Right to Deny the Death Penalty

This conclusion is insupportable as an interpretation of the Constitution, which generally leaves it to democratically elected legislatures rather than courts to decide what makes

Justice Antonin Gregory Scalia, "Justice Scalia, Concurring in Judgment, Supreme Court of the United States, No. 07-5439, Ralph Baze and Thomas C. Bowling, Petitioners v. John D. Rees, Commissioner, Kentucky Department of Corrections, et al.," www.qj supremecourt.gov, pp. 1-8.

significant contribution to social or public purposes. Besides that more general proposition, the very text of the document recognizes that the death penalty is a permissible legislative choice. The Fifth Amendment expressly requires a presentment or indictment of a grand jury to hold a person to answer for "a capital, or otherwise infamous crime," and prohibits deprivation of "life" without due process of law. The same Congress that proposed the Eighth Amendment also enacted the Act of April 30, 1790, which made several offenses punishable by death. Writing in 1976, Professor Hugo Bedau—no friend of the death penalty himself—observed that "[u]ntil fifteen years ago, save for a few mavericks, no one gave any credence to the possibility of ending the death penalty by judicial interpretation of constitutional law." There is simply no legal authority for the proposition that the imposition of death as a criminal penalty is unconstitutional other than the opinions in *Furman v. Georgia* (1972), which established a nationwide moratorium on capital punishment that Justice Stevens had a hand in ending four years later in *Gregg* [*v. Georgia*, 1976].

Justice Stevens' policy analysis of the constitutionality of capital punishment fails on its own terms.

What prompts Justice Stevens to repudiate his prior view and to adopt the astounding position that a criminal sanction expressly mentioned in the Constitution violates the Constitution? His analysis begins with what he believes to be the "uncontroversial legal premise" that the "'extinction of life with only marginal contributions to any discernible social or public purposes ... would be patently excessive' and violative of the Eighth Amendment." Even if that were uncontroversial in the abstract (and it is certainly not what occurs to me as the meaning of "cruel and unusual punishments"), it is assuredly controversial (indeed, flat-out wrong) as applied to a mode of punishment that is explicitly sanctioned by the Constitution.

As to that, *the People* have determined whether there is adequate contribution to social or public purposes, and it is no business of unelected judges to set that judgment aside. But even if we grant Justice Stevens his "uncontroversial premise," his application of that premise to the current practice of capital punishment does not meet the "heavy burden [that] rests on those who would attack the judgment of the representatives of the people." That is to say, Justice Stevens' policy analysis of the constitutionality of capital punishment fails on its own terms.

It is simply not our place to choose one set of responsible empirical studies over another in interpreting the Constitution.

Capital Punishment May Very Well Deter Murder

According to Justice Stevens, the death penalty promotes none of the purposes of criminal punishment because it neither prevents more crimes than alternative measures nor serves a retributive purpose. He argues that "the recent rise in statutes providing for life imprisonment without the possibility of parole" means that States have a ready alternative to the death penalty. Moreover, "[d]espite 30 years of empirical research in the area, there remains no reliable statistical evidence that capital punishment in fact deters potential offenders." Taking the points together, Justice Stevens concludes that the availability of alternatives, and what he describes as the unavailability of "reliable statistical evidence," renders capital punishment unconstitutional. In his view, the benefits of capital punishment—as compared to other forms of punishment such as life imprisonment—are outweighed by the costs.

These conclusions are not supported by the available data. Justice Stevens' analysis barely acknowledges the "significant body of recent evidence that capital punishment may well have a deterrent effect, possibly a quite powerful one" [as written by Cass Sunstein and Adrian Vermeule]. According to a "leading national study," "each execution prevents some eighteen murders, on average." "If the current evidence is even roughly correct ... then a refusal to impose capital punishment will effectively condemn numerous innocent people to death."

Of course, it may well be that the empirical studies establishing that the death penalty has a powerful deterrent effect are incorrect, and some scholars have disputed its deterrent value. But that is not the point. It is simply not our place to choose one set of responsible empirical studies over another in interpreting the Constitution. Nor is it our place to demand that state legislatures support their criminal sanctions with foolproof empirical studies, rather than commonsense predictions about human behavior. "The value of capital punishment as a deterrent of crime is a complex factual issue the resolution of which properly rests with the legislatures, which can evaluate the results of statistical studies in terms of their own local conditions and with a flexibility of approach that is not available to the courts." Were Justice Stevens' current view the constitutional test, even his own preferred criminal sanction—life imprisonment without the possibility of parole—may fail constitutional scrutiny, because it is entirely unclear that enough empirical evidence supports that sanction as compared to alternatives such as life with the possibility of parole.

Capital Punishment Does Serve a Retributive Purpose

But even if Justice Stevens' assertion about the deterrent value of the death penalty were correct, the death penalty would yet be constitutional (as he concedes) if it served the appropriate purpose of retribution. I would think it difficult indeed to prove that a criminal sanction fails to serve a retributive purpose—a judgment that strikes me as inherently subjective and insusceptible of judicial review. Justice Stevens, however, concludes that, because the Eighth Amendment "protect[s] the inmate from enduring any punishment that is comparable to the suffering inflicted on his victim," capital punishment serves no retributive purpose at all. The infliction of any pain, according to Justice Stevens, violates the Eighth Amendment's prohibition against cruel and unusual punishments, but so too does the imposition of capital punishment *without pain* because a criminal penalty lacks a retributive purpose unless it inflicts pain commensurate with the pain that the criminal has caused. In other words, if a punishment is not retributive enough, it is not retributive at all. To state this proposition is to refute it, as Justice Stevens once understood. "[T]he decision that capital punishment may be the appropriate sanction in extreme cases is an expression of the community's belief that certain crimes are themselves so grievous an affront to humanity that the only adequate response may be the penalty of death."

The Risk of Error Is Not Greater in Capital Cases

Justice Stevens' final refuge in his cost-benefit analysis is a familiar one: There is a risk that an innocent person might be convicted and sentenced to death—though not a risk that Justice Stevens can quantify, because he lacks a single example of a person executed for a crime he did not commit in the current American system. His analysis of this risk is thus a series of sweeping condemnations that, if taken seriously, would prevent any punishment under any criminal justice system. According to him, "[t]he prosecutorial concern that death verdicts would rarely be returned by 12 randomly selected jurors should be viewed as objective evidence supporting the conclusion that the penalty is excessive." But prosecutors undoubtedly have a similar concern that *any* unanimous conviction would rarely be returned by 12 randomly selected jurors. That is why they, like defense counsel, are permitted to use the challenges for cause and peremptory challenges that Justice Stevens finds so troubling, in order to arrive at a jury that both sides believe will be more likely to do justice in a particular case. Justice Stevens' concern that prosecutors will be inclined to challenge jurors who will not find a person guilty supports not his conclusion, but the separate (and equally erroneous) conclusion that peremptory challenges and challenges for cause are unconstitutional. According to Justice Stevens, "the risk of error in capital cases may be greater than in other cases because the facts are often so disturbing that the interest in making sure the crime does not go unpunished may overcome residual doubt concerning the identity of the offender." That rationale, however, supports not Justice Stevens' conclusion that the death penalty is unconstitutional, but the more sweeping proposition that any conviction in a case in which facts are disturbing is suspect—including, of course, convictions resulting in life without parole in those States that do not have capital punishment. The same is true of Justice Stevens' claim that there is a risk of "discriminatory application of the death penalty." The same could be said of any criminal penalty, including life without parole; there is no proof that in this regard the death penalty is distinctive.

The People Should Decide—Not the Judges

But of all Justice Stevens' criticisms of the death penalty, the hardest to take is his bemoaning of "the enormous costs that death penalty litigation imposes on society," including the "burden on the courts and the lack of finality for victim's families." Those costs, those burdens, and that lack of finality are in large measure the creation of Justice Stevens and other Justices opposed to the death penalty, who have "encumber[ed] [it] ... with unwarranted restrictions neither contained in the

text of the Constitution nor reflected in two centuries of practice under it"—the product of their policy views "not shared
by the vast majority of the American people."

But actually none of this really matters. As Justice Stevens
explains, "'objective evidence, though of great importance,
[does] not wholly determine the controversy, for the Constitution contemplates that in the end *our own judgment will be
brought to bear on the question of the acceptability of the death
penalty under the Eighth Amendment.'" "I have relied *on my
own experience* in reaching the conclusion that the imposition
of the death penalty" is unconstitutional.

Purer expression cannot be found of the principle of rule
by judicial fiat. In the face of Justice Stevens' experience, the
experience of all others is, it appears, of little consequence.
The experience of the state legislatures and the Congress—
who retain the death penalty as a form of punishment—is
dismissed as "the product of habit and inattention rather than
an acceptable deliberative process." The experience of social
scientists whose studies indicate that the death penalty deters
crime is relegated to a footnote. The experience of fellow citizens who support the death penalty is described, with only
the most thinly veiled condemnation, as stemming from a
"thirst for vengeance." It is Justice Stevens' experience that
reigns over all.

3

Capital Punishment Is Morally Justified

Casey Carmical

Casey Carmical is a professional translator and writes a blog called "Casey's Critical Thinking" regarding current social and political issues.

Despite arguments to the contrary, the death penalty is a morally acceptable punishment for murder. In fact, it is morally wrong not to execute a murderer because punishment must fit the crime. Simply putting someone in jail does not compare to taking someone's life. As to the reasons most often given for abolishing the death penalty—such as the death penalty does not deter crime or the death penalty is unconstitutional—they are easily and rationally refuted. The purpose of the death penalty is to bring the murderer to justice and to acknowledge the sanctity and dignity of innocent human life.

The death penalty has faced much opposition as of late. Can the death penalty possibly be a morally acceptable punishment? A popular bumper sticker says, "We kill people to show people that killing people is wrong." The slogan is short, simple, and to the point. But is there really such irony in capital punishment as the slogan implies?

First of all, the slogan misses an important point. The death penalty does not punish people for killing, but for murder. Killing is justified when it is done in self-defense. Killing means to cause death. Murder, on the other hand, is defined as "the unlawful and malicious or premeditated killing of one human being by another." (For the less observant, this definition cannot be applied to the death penalty, because the death penalty is lawful, non-malicious, and is not carried out by an individual but by the government). "Kill," "murder," and "execute" are not interchangeable terms. Death penalty opponents would like us to believe otherwise. Just because two actions result in the same end does not make them morally equivalent. If it were so, legal incarceration would be equated with kidnapping, lovemaking with rape, self-defense with battery, etc. Therefore, the slogan is better stated, "We execute people to show people that murder is wrong." Not quite as catchy, is it?

Morally, it is wrong to simply incarcerate someone for murder.

Morality

Morality is defined as "the principles of right and wrong." As moral creatures, humans deserve praise for good deeds, and punishment for bad ones. Punishment may range from a slap on the wrist to death, but the punishment must fit the crime. This is known as *lex talionis*, or in common jargon, "an eye for an eye." Abolitionists [those who want to abolish the death penalty] often insist that if we argue for *lex talion* justice we must be prepared to rape rapists, beat sadists, and burn down the houses of arsonists. Certainly, this is the case if we take the *lex talion* literally, and the criminals *do* deserve those punishments, but we needn't take it literally. The ancient Jews did not. They allowed for monetary compensation for physical or property damage.

Why then, if it is not morally okay to rape rapists, is it acceptable to execute murderers? The answer is simple. There is no redeeming value to carrying out the former punishment. Raping the rapist will only cause someone else to degrade themselves by doing it. It will not prevent the rapist from raping again. Executing murderers, however, prevents them from committing their crime again, and thus protects innocent victims. The good, therefore, outweighs the bad, and the executioner is morally justified in taking the murderer's life. On the other hand, if the abolitionist argues that killing is always wrong, then he must also concede that killing in self-defense is unacceptable and should be punished. Few, if any, however, are willing to do so. The abolitionist may choose to argue that the state should never kill. But consider also the scenario of protecting someone else's life. Are police officers (the state) justified in killing attempted murderers to save a victim's life? If the answer to this question is yes, then the question is no longer if the state is justified in taking the life of criminals, but when.

Morally, it is wrong to simply incarcerate someone for murder. A sentence of life in an air-conditioned, cable-equipped prison where a person gets free meals three times a day, personal recreation time, and regular visits with friends and family is a slap in the face of morality. People will say here that not all prisons are like the one cited. This betrays an ignorance, however, of current trends. Eventually, criminal rights activists will see to it that all prisons are nice places to go. But regardless of the conditions of a particular prison, someone who murders another human being can only be made to pay for his actions by forfeiting his own life. This is so, simply because a loss of freedom does not and cannot compare to a loss of life. If the punishment for theft is imprisonment, then the punishment for murder must be exponentially more severe, because human life is infinitely more valuable than any material item.

Take, for example, a murderer who took the life of a teenager. The parents of the victim will be among the taxpayers that pay for his meals and his cable television. Should he choose to take advantage of college courses the prison may offer, the parents of the victim will be indirectly financing those expenses as well. Nothing could be further from justice. It is of this type of situation that the abolitionist approves. Somewhere along the line, their priorities have been turned upside down.

More than Revenge

Abolitionists claim that the death penalty is a means of revenge. It is not. One way for the victim's family to get revenge would be to go out and murder a member of the murderer's family in order to get him to experience the same type of suffering he put them through. If the purpose of the state in executing murderers was retribution or revenge, then criminals would be executed in the same way they that murdered their victims. The point of the death penalty, however, is not to see how much pain can be unleashed on the murderer but to bring him to justice.

In reality, the murderer actually gets off easy when he is sentenced to death in the United States. There are five methods of execution used in the United States: lethal injection, electrocution, lethal gas, hanging, and firing squad. The most commonly used methods today are lethal injection and the electric chair. If a person is lethally injected, he is first put to sleep with thiopental sodium, and then he is administered potassium chloride that will stop his heart. The criminal dies from anesthetic overdose and respiratory and cardiac arrest while he or she is unconscious. As for the electric chair, there is an initial jolt of 2,300 volts (9.5 amps) which lasts for eight seconds, followed by a low-voltage jolt of 1,000 volts (4 amps) for 22 seconds and finally a jolt of 2,300 volts (9.5 amps) for eight seconds. The murderer is rendered unconscious immediately, or within the first eight seconds at most, as the initial high-voltage jolt kills the brain. The subsequent jolts stop the heart in case it is still beating. Compare this to the heinous crimes of the murderer, where often the victim will go through excruciating pain for minutes, hours, or sometimes days. The minute amount of pain experienced by the murderer on death row does not even begin to compensate for the pain of the victims.

Five Reasons to Support the Death Penalty

The Campaign to End the Death Penalty gives five reasons on their website why the death penalty should be abolished. Those reasons are quite commonly given, so I will address their objections here.

1. The death penalty is racist.

2. The death penalty punishes the poor.

These are basically the same argument. What it boils down to is "the death penalty is not applied fairly." This cannot be an argument against the death penalty. If it were, then it would be an argument against *all* punishments. To argue that the death penalty is to be abolished because it is not fairly imposed is to admit that if it were imposed fairly it would be okay. This is not an argument against the death penalty but an argument to improve the justice system. Is the system unfair? Fix it. What is unfair is not that the black and poor prisoners get what they deserve. What is unfair is that the rich and white prisoners do not.

3. The death penalty condemns the innocent to die.

There is absolutely no proof for this statement. Before any person is executed in this country, twelve members of a carefully selected jury have to decide—beyond a reasonable doubt—that a defendant is guilty. The possibility of an innocent person being executed is extremely small, and continues to decrease with the improvement of forensic science. It is true that death row prisoners have been released, but it is not always true that they were innocent.

Consider the following fact: A judgment of acquittal is final. Even if overwhelming evidence is later uncovered, the prosecution can never appeal. A retrial would constitute "double jeopardy" which is not permitted under the Fifth Amendment to the United States Constitution. Likewise, if a conviction is reversed on appeal because the evidence of guilt was *legally* insufficient to prove guilt *beyond a reasonable doubt,* then the defendant cannot be retried. Furthermore, if a court decides that the evidence brought against the defendant was legally insufficient, it is not saying that the defendant was *actually* innocent. By making this decision, the court is merely saying that the prosecution did not prove the defendant's guilt beyond a reasonable doubt.

The death penalty is, without question, a deterrent to murder.

Dudley Sharp [founder of the criminal justice reform organization Justice For All] notes, "It is important to preserve the distinction between acquittal and innocence, which is regularly obfuscated in news media headlines." The media often overlooks this distinction, and thrives on causing widespread panic that an innocent person was falsely convicted. Being acquitted, however, does not mean that the defendant did not actually commit the crime. A jury must acquit "someone who is probably guilty but whose guilt is not established beyond a reasonable doubt." [From] *Gregg v. Georgia,* (1976).

4. The death penalty is not a deterrent against violent crime.

The death penalty as a deterrent to crime is not the issue. Capital punishment is, pardon the redundancy, a punishment for crime. As a punishment, the death penalty is 100% effective—every time it is used, the prisoner dies.

Additionally, the death penalty is actually 100% effective as a deterrent to crime: the murderer will never commit another crime once he has been executed. While there is no proof that any innocents have been executed in this century, there is an abundance of evidence that prisoners who either escaped or were released early murdered innocent victims again. Professor [and former federal judge in Utah] Paul Cassell points out that

> Out of a sample of 164 paroled Georgia murderers, eight committed subsequent murders within seven years of release. A study of twenty Oregon murderers released on parole in 1979 found that one (i.e., five percent) had committed a subsequent homicide within five years of release. Another study found that of 11,404 persons originally convicted of "willful homicide" and released during 1965 and 1974, 34 were returned to prison for commission of a subsequent criminal homicide during the first year alone.

Even those who are not released but still serve life terms murder again. Cassell further notes that, "At least five federal prison officers have been killed since December 1982, and the inmates in at least three of the incidents were already serving life sentences for murder." Had these prisoners been executed, innocent lives would have been saved. The death penalty is, without question, a deterrent to murder.

(Seven recent studies make it clear that executions deter murders and murder rates increase substantially during moratoriums.)

5. The death penalty is cruel and unusual punishment.

The death penalty is not cruel and unusual punishment. The framers of the Constitution supported the death penalty, and in fact constructed laws in order to carry it out, so it is ridiculous to claim that cruel and unusual punishment refers to the death penalty. Justice Antonin Scalia observed, "The Fifth Amendment provides that '[n]o persons shall be held to answer for a capital . . . crime, unless on a presentment or indictment of a Grand Jury . . . nor be deprived of life . . . without the due process of law.' This clearly permits the death penalty to be imposed, and establishes beyond doubt that the death penalty is not one of the 'cruel and unusual punishments' prohibited by the Eighth Amendment."

The American draftsmen were primarily concerned with proscribing "tortures" and other "barbarous" methods of punishment. The U.S. Supreme Court noted in *Gregg v. Georgia* that "In the earliest cases raising Eighth Amendment claims, the Court focused on particular methods of execution to determine whether they were too cruel to pass constitutional muster. The constitutionality of the sentence of death itself was not at issue."

The death penalty is moral and just.

The Senate Judiciary Committee once noted, "[M]urder does not simply differ in magnitude from extortion or burglary or property destruction offenses; it differs in kind. Its punishment ought to also differ in kind. It must acknowledge the inviolability and dignity of innocent human life. It must, in short, be proportionate."

The very notion that one could be cruel while punishing a guilty murderer for murdering an innocent victim is laughable.

Death Penalty Yes, Murder No

I have tried to argue here that the death penalty is moral and just. We must never forget that no one has to be executed; if no one murders, no one is executed. Murderers are not innocent people fighting for their lives; that statement describes their victims. Let us work in America to get back the mentality that victim rights are more important than criminal rights.

4

The Death Penalty Deters Murder

Center for Individual Freedom

Founded in 1998, the Center for Individual Freedom is a nonpartisan, nonprofit organization with the mission to protect and defend individual freedoms and rights guaranteed by the U.S. Constitution.

When discussing moral justification for capital punishment, one of the main issues is whether the death penalty actually deters criminals from committing murder. To answer that question, two professors from Pepperdine University in California conducted a research study, and their results indicated the answer to be yes. In fact, their evidence correlated each execution with approximately seventy-four fewer murders the following year. Therefore, statistical evidence shows that the death penalty does prevent future murders and is thus justified.

In the never-ending debate between capital punishment proponents and abolitionist [people who want to end the death penalty], one ongoing point of contention centers upon whether the death penalty actually deters future murders in America.

According to a new [2007] study by Pepperdine University professors Roy D. Adler and Michael Summers, the answer is an emphatic "yes." Based upon their evidence, capital punishment exerts a demonstrable, significant statistical deterrent impact upon the number of murders in America. As a consequence, their study shifts the burden of persuasion dramatically to abolitionists.

Of course, one should note that even if capital punishment had no demonstrable deterrent effect upon crime or murder in America, several other justifications for its imposition would nevertheless remain.

Deterrence Is One of Four Justifications

The preceding declaration stems from the fact that, according to the heritage of our common law, four philosophical and moral justifications for criminal punishment exist. Deterrence is merely one of those four.

The first justification, which is perhaps most ingrained in basic human nature, is what we commonly know as "retribution." This elementary moral justification asserts that one who commits an illegal or immoral act should himself suffer for having committed that act. Or, in common parlance, "an eye for an eye, a tooth for a tooth." Although some people consider this a vulgar, unfortunate or improper justification for imposing criminal penalties upon other human beings, the simple fact is that it continues to constitute an important basis for criminal law and punishment. Agree or disagree, our society generally believes that a bad deed should not go unpunished.

Society aspires to create a criminal justice system that deters future crimes by making an example of those who commit them.

The second traditional justification for criminal penalties is what we know as "incapacitation." Very simply, this holds that by removing a criminal from society through imprisonment or capital punishment, the criminal is thereby incapacitated from committing additional crimes. Indeed, this partly explains why crime rates in New York City fell so dramatically under the tenure of Mayor Rudy Giuliani. According to his theory, the same small segment of society tended to commit both the seemingly "minor" crimes as well as the "major" crimes. Thus, removing those who committed supposedly "minor" crimes incapacitated them from committing future "major" crimes if allowed to remain on the street, and crime plummeted. In similar fashion, capital punishment serves this incapacitation rationale because it permanently removes our most vicious criminals from society, thereby eliminating any threat of future crime that they pose while in prison, after escape or after parole.

The third of four traditional justifications for criminal law is that of "rehabilitation." In other words, in a perfect world, imposition of criminal penalties would serve to rehabilitate those who commit crime, whether through education in prison, or teaching the more fundamental truism that "crime doesn't pay." Obviously, capital punishment does less to serve this particular justification, apart from the possible improvement that a murderer can undergo between capture and execution.

A Deterrent Relationship Between Executions and Murders

This brings us to the fourth justification for criminal law, and the subject of the eye-opening new study: "deterrence." In other words, society aspires to create a criminal justice system that deters future crimes by making an example of those who commit them.

In turn, this brings us to Professors Adler and Summers, and their remarkable new study. Examining the 26-year period from 1979 to 2004, they correlated the number of executions in America to the number of murders during that span. It became immediately clear that as executions in America increase, murders decrease. Conversely, when executions decreased, murders increased.

In fact, the study revealed that each execution was correlated with some 74 fewer murders the following year.

Obviously, Professors Adler and Summers were concerned that this corollary relationship was merely coincidental. Therefore, they conducted a grueling statistical regression analysis on the relationship. To their surprise, their regression analysis established that the odds against the pattern being random were approximately 18,000 to 1.

Naturally, death penalty opponents will struggle to suggest alternative explanations for this remarkable evidence of capital punishment's deterrent effect, such as increased police activity, economic prosperity or perhaps demographic shifts. In light of the professors' new study, however, such opponents now carry a much heavier burden of proof in refuting this dramatic deterrent relationship.

Even more fundamentally, death penalty opponents now carry a heavier burden to explain why sparing the life of a convicted murderer somehow outweighs sparing the lives of dozens of future murder victims.

Let the debate continue on this powerful new note.

5

The Death Penalty Has Not Been Proven to Deter Murder

Jeremy J. Collins

Jeremy J. Collins, the director of the North Carolina Coalition for a Moratorium (NCCM), works in the nonprofit sector educating and mobilizing citizens while providing grassroots and legislative advocacy for social justice issues.

Some research studies claim to have proven that the death penalty has a deterrent impact on murder. Leading academics and experts, however, debunk such claims and explain that socioeconomic, crime rate, and criminal justice system variables are too complex to prove a valid deterrent effect. Furthermore, evidence has shown that murder rates are lower in states without the death penalty, and a separate study found that in thirteen states with the death penalty, the murder rate was actually higher.

Though most experts have long dismissed any measurable deterrent effect from the use of the death penalty, a recent AP [Associated Press] story helped spark new discussion on the topic.

According to the report, some academic studies have purported to find such a deterrent impact. The story cited a 2003 Emory University study which concluded that each execution deters an average of 18 murders. To read the story, one might believe that new life has been pumped into what had largely been a settled argument.

Jeremy J. Collins, "Death Penalty No Deterrent to Murder," *The Carrboro Citizen*, July 19, 2007. Copyright © 2007 by The Carrboro Citizen. Reproduced by permission.

Experts Reject the Deterrence Claim

A closer look at the facts, however, reveals that there was very little to the story. The truth is that leading academics have roundly rejected these studies. A rigorous 2006 study conducted by John Donohue of Yale Law School and the National Bureau of Economic Research (NBER) and Justin Wolfers of the Wharton School of Business and NBER analyzed the same data used in the Emory study and like studies and debunked their conclusions in striking terms: "The view that the death penalty deters is still the product of belief, not evidence." In fact, the researchers found that, if anything, "the evidence suggests that the death penalty may increase the murder rate."

Studies finding a deterrent effect are "fraught with numerous technical and conceptual errors."

These dueling findings have a deja vu quality. The studies purporting to find a deterrent effect all build upon the foundation of a 1975 article in which Prof. Isaac Ehrlich claimed that each execution averted eight murders. Economists and social scientists attempted to replicate his findings by using different data and improving on his methodology. The overwhelming majority of such studies found no evidence that the death penalty deters murderers. Indeed, a 1978 panel of experts appointed by the National Academy of Sciences strongly criticized Ehrlich's work and methodology.

Jeffrey Fagan, a professor at Columbia Law School and an expert on statistics, testified before Congress that the Emory study and similar Ehrlich-inspired studies finding a deterrent effect are "fraught with numerous technical and conceptual errors." Important among these problems is that the studies "avoid any direct tests of deterrence." That road would likely not lead to deterrence findings: numerous studies "show the limits of the assumptions or rationality that underlie deterrence" while others show the cognitive, organic and neuropsychological impairments which characterize violent offenders.

Instead of attempting a direct test of deterrence, the Ehrlich-inspired studies acknowledge that the factors leading a person to murder (or not murder) are complex and numerous—including socioeconomic variables, crime rates and the efficacy of the criminal justice system in catching, convicting and punishing criminals. The studies purport to isolate every other factor but the availability of the death penalty as punishment for murder. But common sense and respected scientists such as Profs. Donahue and Wolfers tell us that the number of homicides that executions "can plausibly have caused or deterred cannot be reliably disentangled from the large year-to-year changes in the homicide rate caused by other factors."

Evidence Contradicts the Deterrence Claim

When touting superficially powerful arguments in favor of the state executing our fellow human beings, the media and academics have a duty to acknowledge the facts contradicting their claims. These facts include not only that respected academics have rejected claims that the death penalty deters, but also the following:

- Murder rates are lower in states without the death penalty. This holds true even when comparing neighboring states.

- While Southern states account for over 80 percent of the executions in this country, they have consistently had the highest murder rate of the nation's four regions.

- Since 1972, homicide rates in Canada and the United States have moved in lockstep, yet in that period, Canada has not executed a single person and the United States has executed over 1,000 people. When homicides go down in the United States, they go down in Canada, even though Canada does not use capital punishment.

- One of the authors of the Emory study (Joanna Shepherd) found in a separate study that while the death penalty deterred murder in six states, it actually increased murder in 13 states and had no effect on the murder rate in eight states. Other studies have found that the death penalty has a "brutalization effect," increasing the number of murders.

Danger lurks whenever we look at statistical claims without a skeptical eye, never more so than when the issue is life and death. We need straight information before making an informed decision on the death penalty. Statistical claims that wilt under the mildest scrutiny woefully fail to meet that test.

6

Capital Punishment Should Never Be Considered in Child Rape Cases

Justice Anthony McLeod Kennedy

Appointed by President Ronald Reagan in 1988, Anthony McLeod Kennedy is an Associate Justice of the US Supreme Court.

Patrick Kennedy was charged by the state of Louisiana with aggravated rape of his eight-year-old stepdaughter in 1998, and a jury sentenced him to death. Kennedy appealed his death sentence to the US Supreme Court, citing the US Constitution's Eighth Amendment prohibition of excessive or cruel and unusual punishment. After hearing the case, the Supreme Court determined that the Eighth Amendment prohibits the death penalty for the offense of raping a child because of the risk that child testimony might be unreliable or untrue, because punishing child rapists with the death penalty might create an incentive for the rapist to kill the victim, and because capital punishment should be limited to offenders who commit the most serious of crimes— murder.

The National Government and, beyond it, the separate States are bound by the proscriptive mandates of the Eighth Amendment to the Constitution of the United States, and all persons within those respective jurisdictions may invoke its protection. Patrick Kennedy, the petitioner here, seeks

Justice Anthony McLeod Kennedy, "Supreme Court of the United States, No. 07-343, Patrick Kennedy, Petitioner v. Louisiana," June 25, 2008.

to set aside his death sentence under the Eighth Amendment. He was charged by the respondent, the State of Louisiana, with the aggravated rape of his then-8-year-old stepdaughter. After a jury trial, petitioner was convicted and sentenced to death under a state statute authorizing capital punishment for the rape of a child under 12 years of age. This case presents the question whether the Constitution bars respondent from imposing the death penalty for the rape of a child where the crime did not result, and was not intended to result, in death of the victim. We hold the Eighth Amendment prohibits the death penalty for this offense. The Louisiana statute is unconstitutional. . . .

A death sentence for one who raped but did not kill a child . . . is unconstitutional under the Eighth and Fourteenth Amendments.

Limitations Under the Eighth Amendment

The Eighth Amendment, applicable to the States through the Fourteenth Amendment, provides that "[e]xcessive bail shall not be required, nor excessive fines imposed, nor cruel and unusual punishments inflicted." The Amendment proscribes "all excessive punishments, as well as cruel and unusual punishments that may or may not be excessive." . . .

Evolving standards of decency must embrace and express respect for the dignity of the person, and the punishment of criminals must conform to that rule. As we shall discuss, punishment is justified under one or more of three principal rationales: rehabilitation, deterrence, and retribution. It is the last of these, retribution, that most often can contradict the law's own ends. This is of particular concern when the Court interprets the meaning of the Eighth Amendment in capital cases. When the law punishes by death, it risks its own sudden descent into brutality, transgressing the constitutional commitment to decency and restraint.

For these reasons we have explained that capital punishment must "be limited to those offenders who commit 'a narrow category of the most serious crimes' and whose extreme culpability makes them 'the most deserving of execution.'". . .

Based both on consensus and our own independent judgment, our holding is that a death sentence for one who raped but did not kill a child, and who did not intend to assist another in killing the child, is unconstitutional under the Eighth and Fourteenth Amendments. . . .

A Disproportionate Penalty for the Crime of Rape

Louisiana is the only State since 1964 that has sentenced an individual to death for the crime of child rape; and petitioner and Richard Davis, who was convicted and sentenced to death for the aggravated rape of a 5-year-old child by a Louisiana jury in December 2007, see *State* v. *Davis*, Case No. 262,971 (1st Jud. Dist., Caddo Parish, La.), are the only two individuals now on death row in the United States for a nonhomicide offense.

After reviewing the authorities informed by contemporary norms, including the history of the death penalty for this and other nonhomicide crimes, current state statutes and new enactments, and the number of executions since 1964, we conclude there is a national consensus against capital punishment for the crime of child rape. . . .

Rape has a permanent psychological, emotional, and sometimes physical impact on the child. We cannot dismiss the years of long anguish that must be endured by the victim of child rape.

It does not follow, though, that capital punishment is a proportionate penalty for the crime. The constitutional prohibition against excessive or cruel and unusual punishments mandates that the State's power to punish "be exercised within the limits of civilized standards." Evolving standards of decency that mark the progress of a maturing society counsel us to be most hesitant before interpreting the Eighth Amendment to allow the extension of the death penalty, a hesitation that has special force where no life was taken in the commission of the crime. It is an established principle that decency, in its essence, presumes respect for the individual and thus moderation or restraint in the application of capital punishment.

To date the Court has sought to define and implement this principle, for the most part, in cases involving capital murder. One approach has been to insist upon general rules that ensure consistency in determining who receives a death sentence. At the same time the Court has insisted, to ensure restraint and moderation in use of capital punishment, on judging the "character and record of the individual offender and the circumstances of the particular offense as a constitutionally indispensable part of the process of inflicting the penalty of death."

The tension between general rules and case-specific circumstances has produced results not all together satisfactory. This has led some Members of the Court to say we should cease efforts to resolve the tension and simply allow legislatures, prosecutors, courts, and juries greater latitude. For others the failure to limit these same imprecisions by stricter enforcement of narrowing rules has raised doubts concerning the constitutionality of capital punishment itself.

Our response to this case law, which is still in search of a unifying principle, has been to insist upon confining the instances in which capital punishment may be imposed.

Our concern here is limited to crimes against individual persons. We do not address, for example, crimes defining and punishing treason, espionage, terrorism, and drug kingpin activity, which are offenses against the State. As it relates to crimes against individuals, though, the death penalty should not be expanded to instances where the victim's life was not taken. We said in *Coker* [*v. Georgia*, 1977] of adult rape:

> We do not discount the seriousness of rape as a crime. It is highly reprehensible, both in a moral sense and in its almost total contempt for the personal integrity and autonomy of the female victim. . . . Short of homicide, it is the "ultimate violation of self." . . . [But] [t]he murderer kills; the rapist, if no more than that, does not. . . . We have the abiding conviction that the death penalty, which "is unique in its severity and irrevocability," is an excessive penalty for the rapist who, as such, does not take human life.

The same distinction between homicide and other serious violent offenses against the individual informed the Court's analysis in *Enmund* [*v. Florida*, 1982], where the Court held that the death penalty for the crime of vicarious felony murder [murder committed by an accomplice during the course of committing another felony] is disproportionate to the offense. The Court repeated there the fundamental, moral distinction between a "murderer" and a "robber," noting that while "robbery is a serious crime deserving serious punishment," it is not like death in its "severity and irrevocability."

Consistent with evolving standards of decency and the teachings of our precedents we conclude that, in determining whether the death penalty is excessive, there is a distinction between intentional first-degree murder on the one hand and nonhomicide crimes against individual persons, even including child rape, on the other. The latter crimes may be devastating in their harm, as here, but "in terms of moral depravity and of the injury to the person and to the public," they cannot be compared to murder in their "severity and irrevocability."

Evolving Standards of Decency

In reaching our conclusion we find significant the number of executions that would be allowed under respondent's approach. The crime of child rape, considering its reported incidents, occurs more often than first-degree murder. Approximately 5,702 incidents of vaginal, anal, or oral rape of a child under the age of 12 were reported nationwide in 2005; this is almost twice the total incidents of intentional murder for victims of all ages (3,405) reported during the same period. Although we have no reliable statistics on convictions for child rape, we can surmise that, each year, there are hundreds, or more, of these convictions just in jurisdictions that permit capital punishment. As a result of existing rules, only 2.2% of convicted first-degree murderers are sentenced to death. But under respondent's approach, the 36 States that permit the death penalty could sentence to death all persons convicted of raping a child less than 12 years of age. This could not be reconciled with our evolving standards of decency and the necessity to constrain the use of the death penalty.

It might be said that narrowing aggravators could be used in this context, as with murder offenses, to ensure the death penalty's restrained application. We find it difficult to identify standards that would guide the decisionmaker so the penalty is reserved for the most severe cases of child rape and yet not imposed in an arbitrary way. Even were we to forbid, say, the execution of first-time child rapists, or require as an aggravating factor a finding that the perpetrator's instant rape offense involved multiple victims, the jury still must balance, in its discretion, those aggravating factors against mitigating circumstances. In this context, which involves a crime that in many cases will overwhelm a decent person's judgment, we have no confidence that the imposition of the death penalty would not be so arbitrary as to be "freakis[h]." We cannot sanction this result when the harm to the victim, though grave, cannot be quantified in the same way as death of the victim.

It is not a solution simply to apply to this context the aggravating factors developed for capital murder. The Court has said that a State may carry out its obligation to ensure individualized sentencing in capital murder cases by adopting sentencing processes that rely upon the jury to exercise wide discretion so long as there are narrowing factors that have some "'common-sense core of meaning . . . that criminal juries should be capable of understanding.'" The Court, accordingly, has upheld the constitutionality of aggravating factors ranging from whether the defendant was a "'cold-blooded, pitiless slayer,'" to whether the "perpetrator inflict[ed] mental anguish or physical abuse before the victim's death," to whether the defendant "'would commit criminal acts of violence that would constitute a continuing threat to society.'" All of these standards have the potential to result in some inconsistency of application.

Evolving standards of decency are difficult to reconcile with a regime that seeks to expand the death penalty.

As noted above, the resulting imprecision and the tension between evaluating the individual circumstances and consistency of treatment have been tolerated where the victim dies. It should not be introduced into our justice system, though, where death has not occurred.

Our concerns are all the more pronounced where, as here, the death penalty for this crime has been most infrequent. We have developed a foundational jurisprudence in the case of capital murder to guide the States and juries in imposing the death penalty. Starting with *Gregg* [*v. Georgia*, 1976], we have spent more than 32 years articulating limiting factors that channel the jury's discretion to avoid the death penalty's arbitrary imposition in the case of capital murder. Though that practice remains sound, beginning the same process for crimes for which no one has been executed in more than 40 years would require experimentation in an area where a failed experiment would result in the execution of individuals undeserving of the death penalty. Evolving standards of decency are difficult to reconcile with a regime that seeks to expand the death penalty to an area where standards to confine its use are indefinite and obscure.

Measuring Retribution and Deterrence

Our decision is consistent with the justifications offered for the death penalty. *Gregg* instructs that capital punishment is excessive when it is grossly out of proportion to the crime or it does not fulfill the two distinct social purposes served by the death penalty: retribution and deterrence of capital crimes.

As in *Coker*, here it cannot be said with any certainty that the death penalty for child rape serves no deterrent or retributive function. . . . This argument does not overcome other objections, however. The incongruity between the crime of child rape and the harshness of the death penalty poses risks of overpunishment and counsels against a constitutional ruling that the death penalty can be expanded to include this offense.

The goal of retribution, which reflects society's and the victim's interests in seeing that the offender is repaid for the hurt he caused, does not justify the harshness of the death penalty here. In measuring retribution, as well as other objectives of criminal law, it is appropriate to distinguish between a particularly depraved murder that merits death as a form of retribution and the crime of child rape.

There is an additional reason for our conclusion that imposing the death penalty for child rape would not further retributive purposes. In considering whether retribution is served, among other factors we have looked to whether capital punishment "has the potential . . . to allow the community as a whole, including the surviving family and friends of the victim, to affirm its own judgment that the culpability of the prisoner is so serious that the ultimate penalty must be sought and imposed." In considering the death penalty for nonhomicide offenses this inquiry necessarily also must include the question whether the death penalty balances the wrong to the victim.

It is not at all evident that the child rape victim's hurt is lessened when the law permits the death of the perpetrator. Capital cases require a long-term commitment by those who testify for the prosecution, especially when guilt and sentencing determinations are in multiple proceedings. In cases like this the key testimony is not just from the family but from the victim herself. . . .

There are, moreover, serious systemic concerns in prosecuting the crime of child rape that are relevant to the constitutionality of making it a capital offense. The problem of unreliable, induced, and even imagined child testimony means there is a "special risk of wrongful execution" in some child rape cases. This undermines, at least to some degree, the meaningful contribution of the death penalty to legitimate goals of punishment. Studies conclude that children are highly susceptible to suggestive questioning techniques like repetition, guided imagery, and selective reinforcement. . . .

A state that punishes child rape by death may remove a strong incentive for the rapist not to kill the victim.

Similar criticisms pertain to other cases involving child witnesses; but child rape cases present heightened concerns because the central narrative and account of the crime often comes from the child herself. She and the accused are, in most instances, the only ones present when the crime was committed. And the question in a capital case is not just the fact of the crime, including, say, proof of rape as distinct from abuse short of rape, but details bearing upon brutality in its commission. These matters are subject to fabrication or exaggeration, or both. Although capital punishment does bring retribution, and the legislature here has chosen to use it for this end, its judgment must be weighed, in deciding the constitutional question, against the special risks of unreliable testimony with respect to this crime.

With respect to deterrence, if the death penalty adds to the risk of non-reporting, that, too, diminishes the penalty's objectives. Underreporting is a common problem with respect to child sexual abuse. . . . Although we know little about what differentiates those who report from those who do not report, one of the most commonly cited reasons for nondisclosure is fear of negative consequences for the perpetrator, a concern that has special force where the abuser is a family member. . . . The experience of the *amici* [uninvolved experts who are permitted to advise the court] who work with child victims indicates that, when the punishment is death, both the victim and the victim's family members may be more likely to shield the perpetrator from discovery, thus increasing underreporting. As a result, punishment by death may not result in more deterrence or more effective enforcement.

In addition, by in effect making the punishment for child rape and murder equivalent, a State that punishes child rape by death may remove a strong incentive for the rapist not to kill the victim. Assuming the offender behaves in a rational way, as one must to justify the penalty on grounds of deterrence, the penalty in some respects gives less protection, not more, to the victim, who is often the sole witness to the crime. It might be argued that, even if the death penalty results in a marginal increase in the incentive to kill, this is counterbalanced by a marginally increased deterrent to commit the crime at all. Whatever balance the legislature strikes, however, uncertainty on the point makes the argument for the penalty less compelling than for homicide crimes.

Each of these propositions, standing alone, might not establish the unconstitutionality of the death penalty for the crime of child rape. Taken in sum, however, they demonstrate the serious negative consequences of making child rape a capital offense. These considerations lead us to conclude, in our independent judgment, that the death penalty is not a proportional punishment for the rape of a child.

7

Capital Punishment Should Be Considered in Certain Child Rape Cases

Justice Samuel Anthony Alito

Nominated by President George W. Bush, Samuel Anthony Alito, Jr., has served as an Associate Justice of the Supreme Court of the United States since January 31, 2006.

On June 25, 2008, the Supreme Court of the United States determined that the Eighth Amendment to the US Constitution prohibits the death penalty from being imposed for raping a child. The reasons for reaching that determination, however, are not valid. For example, the Supreme Court stated that permitting the death penalty in child-rape cases is not in the best interests of the victims or society and could, in fact, create an incentive for the rapist to kill the victim. The Court's arguments are not pertinent to the Eighth Amendment, nor are the concerns regarding the reliability of evidence and child testimony in child-rape cases. Furthermore, rapists who inflict lifelong physical and emotional injury on defenseless children cause sufficient grievous harm to warrant receiving the punishment of death.

The Court today [June 25, 2008], holds that the Eighth Amendment categorically prohibits the imposition of the death penalty for the crime of raping a child. This is so, according to the Court, no matter how young the child, no matter how many times the child is raped, no matter how many

Justice Samuel Anthony Alito, "Supreme Court of the United States, No. 07-343, Patrick Kennedy, Petitioner *v.* Louisiana," June 25, 2008.

children the perpetrator rapes, no matter how sadistic the crime, no matter how much physical or psychological trauma is inflicted, and no matter how heinous the perpetrator's prior criminal record may be. The Court provides two reasons for this sweeping conclusion: First, the Court claims to have identified "a national consensus" that the death penalty is never acceptable for the rape of a child; second, the Court concludes, based on its "independent judgment," that imposing the death penalty for child rape is inconsistent with "'the evolving standards of decency that mark the progress of a maturing society.'" . . .

A major theme of the Court's opinion is that permitting the death penalty in child-rape cases is not in the best interests of the victims of these crimes and society at large. In this vein, the Court suggests that it is more painful for child-rape victims to testify when the prosecution is seeking the death penalty. The Court also argues that "a State that punishes child rape by death may remove a strong incentive for the rapist not to kill the victim," and may discourage the reporting of child rape.

These policy arguments, whatever their merits, are simply not pertinent to the question whether the death penalty is "cruel and unusual" punishment. The Eighth Amendment protects the right of an accused. It does not authorize this Court to strike down federal or state criminal laws on the ground that they are not in the best interests of crime victims or the broader society. The Court's policy arguments concern matters that legislators should—and presumably do—take into account in deciding whether to enact a capital child-rape statute, but these arguments are irrelevant to the question that is before us in this case. Our cases have cautioned against using "'the aegis of the Cruel and Unusual Punishment Clause' to cut off the normal democratic processes," but the Court forgets that warning here.

Restrictions for Imposing the Death Penalty

The Court also contends that laws permitting the death penalty for the rape of a child create serious procedural problems. Specifically, the Court maintains that it is not feasible to channel the exercise of sentencing discretion in child-rape cases, and that the unreliability of the testimony of child victims creates a danger that innocent defendants will be convicted and executed. Neither of these contentions provides a basis for striking down all capital child-rape laws no matter how carefully and narrowly they are crafted.

The Court's argument regarding the structuring of sentencing discretion is hard to comprehend. The Court finds it "difficult to identify standards that would guide the decision-maker so the penalty is reserved for the most severe cases of child rape and yet not imposed in an arbitrary way." Even assuming that the age of a child is not alone a sufficient factor for limiting sentencing discretion, the Court need only examine the child-rape laws recently enacted in Texas, Oklahoma, Montana, and South Carolina, all of which use a concrete factor to limit quite drastically the number of cases in which the death penalty may be imposed. In those States, a defendant convicted of the rape of a child may be sentenced to death only if the defendant has a prior conviction for a specified felony sex offense. . . .

Moreover, it takes little imagination to envision other limiting factors that a State could use to structure sentencing discretion in child rape cases. Some of these might be: whether the victim was kidnapped, whether the defendant inflicted severe physical injury on the victim, whether the victim was raped multiple times, whether the rapes occurred over a specified extended period, and whether there were multiple victims.

The Court refers to limiting standards that are "indefinite and obscure," but there is nothing indefinite or obscure about any of the above-listed aggravating factors. Indeed, they are far more definite and clear-cut than aggravating factors that we have found to be adequate in murder cases. . . . For these reasons, concerns about limiting sentencing discretion provide no support for the Court's blanket condemnation of all capital child-rape statutes.

This court has not held that capital child rape laws are unconstitutional.

That sweeping holding is also not justified by the Court's concerns about the reliability of the testimony of child victims. First, the Eighth Amendment provides a poor vehicle for addressing problems regarding the admissibility or reliability of evidence, and problems presented by the testimony of child victims are not unique to capital cases. Second, concerns about the reliability of the testimony of child witnesses are not present in every child-rape case. In the case before us, for example, there was undisputed medical evidence that the victim was brutally raped, as well as strong independent evidence that petitioner was the perpetrator. Third, if the Court's evidentiary concerns have Eighth Amendment relevance, they could be addressed by allowing the death penalty in only those child-rape cases in which the independent evidence is sufficient to prove all the elements needed for conviction and imposition of a death sentence. There is precedent for requiring special corroboration in certain criminal cases. For example, some jurisdictions do not allow a conviction based on the uncorroborated testimony of an accomplice. A State wishing to permit the death penalty in child-rape cases could impose an analogous corroboration requirement.

Not an Expansion of the Death Penalty

After all the arguments noted above are put aside, what is left? What remaining grounds does the Court provide to justify its independent judgment that the death penalty for child rape is categorically unacceptable? I see two.

The first is the proposition that we should be "most hesitant before interpreting the Eighth Amendment to allow the *extension* of the death penalty." . . . But holding that the Eighth Amendment does not categorically prohibit the death penalty for the rape of a young child would not "extend" or "expand" the death penalty. Laws enacted by the state legislatures are presumptively constitutional. . . . and until today, this court has not held that capital child rape laws are unconstitutional. Consequently, upholding the constitutionality of such a law would not "extend" or "expand" the death penalty; rather, it would confirm the status of presumptive constitutionality that such laws have enjoyed up to this point. And in any event, this Court has previously made it clear that "[t]he Eighth Amendment is not a ratchet, whereby a temporary consensus on leniency for a particular crime fixes a permanent constitutional maximum, disabling States from giving effect to altered beliefs and responding to changed social conditions."

Degree of Moral Depravity and Harm

The Court's final—and, it appears, principal—justification for its holding is that murder, the only crime for which defendants have been executed since this Court's 1976 death penalty decisions, is unique in its moral depravity and in the severity of the injury that it inflicts on the victim and the public. But the Court makes little attempt to defend these conclusions.

Rape has a permanent psychological, emotional, and sometimes physical impact on the child.

With respect to the question of moral depravity, is it really true that every person who is convicted of capital murder and sentenced to death is more morally depraved than every child rapist? Consider the following two cases. In the first, a defendant robs a convenience store and watches as his accomplice shoots the store owner. The defendant acts recklessly, but was not the triggerman and did not intend the killing. In the second case, a previously convicted child rapist kidnaps, repeatedly rapes, and tortures multiple child victims. Is it clear that the first defendant is more morally depraved than the second? . . .

Indeed, I have little doubt that, in the eyes of ordinary Americans, the very worst child rapists—predators who seek out and inflict serious physical and emotional injury on defenseless young children—are the epitome of moral depravity.

With respect to the question of the harm caused by the rape of child in relation to the harm caused by murder, it is certainly true that the loss of human life represents a unique harm, but that does not explain why other grievous harms are insufficient to permit a death sentence. And the Court does not take the position that no harm other than the loss of life is sufficient. The Court takes pains to limit its holding to "crimes against individual persons" and to exclude "offenses against the State," a category that the Court stretches—without explanation—to include "drug kingpin activity." But the Court makes no effort to explain why the harm caused by such crimes is necessarily greater than the harm caused by the rape of young children. This is puzzling in light of the Court's acknowledgment that "[r]ape has a permanent psychological, emotional, and sometimes physical impact on the child." As the Court aptly recognizes, "[w]e cannot dismiss the years of long anguish that must be endured by the victim of child rape."

The rape of any victim inflicts great injury, and "[s]ome victims are so grievously injured physically or psychologically that life *is* beyond repair." "The immaturity and vulnerability of a child, both physically and psychologically, adds a devastating dimension to rape that is not present when an adult is raped." Long-term studies show that sexual abuse is "grossly intrusive in the lives of children and is harmful to their normal psychological, emotional and sexual development in ways which no just or humane society can tolerate."

It has been estimated that as many as 40% of 7-to-13-year-old sexual assault victims are considered "seriously disturbed." Psychological problems include sudden school failure, unprovoked crying, dissociation, depression, insomnia, sleep disturbances, nightmares, feelings of guilt and inferiority, and self-destructive behavior, including an increased incidence of suicide.

The deep problems that afflict child-rape victims often become society's problems as well. Commentators have noted correlations between childhood sexual abuse and later problems such as substance abuse, dangerous sexual behaviors or dysfunction, inability to relate to others on an interpersonal level, and psychiatric illness. Victims of child rape are nearly 5 times more likely than nonvictims to be arrested for sex crimes and nearly 30 times more likely to be arrested for prostitution.

The harm that is caused to the victims and to society at large by the worst child rapists is grave. It is the judgment of the Louisiana lawmakers and those in an increasing number of other States that these harms justify the death penalty. The Court provides no cogent explanation why this legislative judgment should be overridden. Conclusory references to "decency," "moderation," "restraint," "full progress," and "moral judgment" are not enough.

8

Legislation Will Help Prevent Racial Bias in Death Penalty Convictions

Desiree Evans

Desiree Evans is a contributing writer for Facing South, *the on-line magazine of the Institute for Southern Studies.*

Civil rights groups and several academic studies have long held that racial bias permeates the justice system in the United States, particularly in death penalty cases. For example, a study conducted by two University of North Carolina professors and published by the Common Sense Foundation found that black defendants were twice as likely to receive the death penalty as whites after committing identical crimes. The Racial Justice Act would allow death penalty defendants and death-row inmates to cite statistics to demonstrate that their cases involved racial bias and, therefore, should not have the death penalty applied.

Following a heated and emotional debate on racial disparities in the criminal justice system, the North Carolina House of Representatives on Tuesday [July 14, 2009] narrowly endorsed the Racial Justice Act, legislation that would give capital murder defendants and death row inmates the right to challenge prosecutions on grounds of racial bias.

The Racial Justice Act

Specifically, the Racial Justice Act would allow defendants in death-penalty cases to use statistics to try to show that race played a factor in the application of the death penalty in their cases. If the statistics showed significant racial disparities in how the death penalty has been applied, a judge could block a prosecutor from pursuing the death penalty in that case, or overturn a jury's decision to impose a death sentence. It would also allow inmates currently on death row the opportunity to argue that their death sentences were racially motivated. If a death sentence were thrown out under the bill, it would be converted to a sentence of life in prison without parole.

The act is a landmark piece of legislation for a state where blacks make up 20 percent of the total population but 60 percent of those on death row. The timing is also critical as North Carolina continues to debate the future of capital punishment.

North Carolina has more than 160 inmates currently on death row, although the state's last execution was in August 2006. The hiatus on executions stemmed from several court challenges to the use of lethal injection. Recent court decisions have mostly resolved the remaining legal obstacles to reinstating the practice, such as the May 1 [2009] decision by the North Carolina Supreme Court in a lawsuit between the NC Medical Board and the NC Department of Corrections. The court said that the NC Medical Board overstepped its power with a threat to discipline doctors who participate in executions.

Profound Racial Bias

Civil rights groups like the North Carolina NAACP [National Association for the Advancement of Colored People] have pushed for the NC Racial Justice Act for more than three years, underscoring that the state has profound racial disparities in the application of the death penalty. Between 2007 and 2008, three African-American men on North Carolina's death row—Jonathan Hoffman, Glen Edward Chapman and Levon Jones—were exonerated. In all of the cases, at least one of the murder victims was white. One of the exonerated men was even convicted with an all-white jury. Combined they spent almost 40 years awaiting their executions for crimes they did not commit.

Black defendants in the state were also twice as likely to receive a death sentence when comparing identical crimes.

Only one other state—Kentucky—has a similar Racial Justice Act, although several states have debated similar legislation.

Nationwide, more than 130 death row inmates have been exonerated for wrongful or erroneous convictions since 1973, including eight in North Carolina. Supporters of the Racial Justice Act cite numerous studies that show clear links between race and how the death penalty is applied.

As the *Independent Weekly* reported [May 13, 2009]:

Race can determine whether a defendant who is guilty spends life in prison or is sentenced to death. The American Bar Association, which has recommended temporary moratoriums until states can resolve widespread inconsistencies in death penalty cases, states on its Web site that "Racial and ethnic bias infects the decisions as to who gets prosecuted and who gets sentenced to death."

Amnesty International has found that 79 percent of homicide cases resulting in a death penalty involved a white victim, though half of all homicide victims in the United States are black. And a 2001 study conducted by two University of North Carolina professors, which analyzed cases over a four-year period in the 1990s, found the odds of receiving a death sentence in North Carolina grew 3.5 times in cases where the victim was white. That study, published by the Common Sense Foundation, found that black defendants in the state were also twice as likely to receive a death sentence, when comparing identical crimes. Of the 206 defendants who are on death row or have been executed in North Carolina since 1977, 100—or 49 percent—are black, although the state has had an African-American population of roughly 22 percent over the past three decades.

The NC Racial Justice Act goes to a second vote in the state House today [July 15, 2009], and then it will move back to the state Senate, where it faces a difficult challenge. Observers expect the bill will go into conference committee, where House and Senate negotiators would try to work out a compromise bill that could pass in both chambers. The Senate previously approved a version of the Racial Justice Act in May, but it contained controversial clauses meant to resume the death penalty in North Carolina. Those clauses were later removed in the House.

9

Legislation Will Not Help Prevent Racial Bias in Death Penalty Convictions

Tara Servatius

Tara Servatius is a journalist and a talk-radio host in Charlotte, North Carolina.

In August 2009, North Carolina's Governor Beverly Perdue signed into law the Racial Justice Act, which was supposed to ensure that no person would be racially discriminated against in application of the death penalty. The outcome of this law, however, will be a lower standard of justice in death penalty cases because statistics will be the focus instead of the actual evidence. For example, if any murderer can show a pattern of death penalty verdicts with similar racial circumstances to his own case, he can use the Racial Justice Act to get out of the death penalty, regardless of how persuasive the evidence against him and how brutal and premeditated the crime. The Racial Justice Act will set a precedent for racial injustice.

Suppose the state legislature came up with the harebrained idea to pass a law to exempt the killers of white women from the death penalty, no matter how brutal and premeditated the crime. Kill a black woman, though, and you'd still be looking at possible capital punishment.

There's no way legislators would do something that stupid, you say. The governor, a white woman herself, would never sign it.

Tara Servatius, "Playing Racial-Justice Roulette," *Creative Loafing Charlotte*, November 17, 2009. Copyright © 2009 by Creative Loafing Charlotte. Reproduced by permission.

Theoretical Discrimination Instead of Actual Discrimination

Well, it appears she did. It's called the Racial Justice Act [RJA], and it became Law [in North Carolina] in August [2009] with Gov. Bev Perdue's signature. It goes far beyond barring racial discrimination in capital cases, proof of which was already enough to challenge a death row sentence. It set up a bizarre reverse affirmative action system for the death penalty based not on actual discrimination, but on theoretical discrimination.

All an ax murderer now has to do is to make a mathematically sound statistical argument that the death penalty is handed out more frequently to people of his race in his county, prosecutorial district, or the state. Or he could argue that there was a statistical pattern of outcomes in cases with racial circumstances similar to his that made getting the death penalty more likely. He wouldn't have to prove there was actually any discrimination in his own case.

The law was written to decrease the number of black men on the state's death row—to hell with their victims—and the NAACP [National Association for the Advancement of Colored People] lobbied hard for it. But statistics are funny things, and, as I warned for more than a year before the law's passage, virtually anyone of any race could potentially use it to get out of a death sentence.

Statistics Instead of Justice

Enter Sgt. Richard D. Smith. He convinced a second Fort Bragg [North Carolina] soldier to kill his wife, Sgt. Christina Smith, in 2008. According to an article in the *Fayetteville Observer*, Smith lured his wife into a trap near their home and then watched as his accomplice stabbed her to death.

In a meeting before a Cumberland County judge recently, the *Observer* reported, Smith's lawyer revealed he planned to use the Racial Justice Act to get his client out of the death penalty. Because Christina Smith was white, statistically Richard Smith has a higher chance of getting the death penalty in North Carolina. One problem. Richard Smith is also white. So is his accomplice. But if they can prove that a white man who kills a white woman has a higher chance of getting the death penalty than one who kills a woman of another race, which statistically appears to be the case, Smith may face life in prison instead if convicted of first-degree murder. Worse yet, other men who kill white women, regardless of their race, might then have legal standing to claim the same thing.

Anthony Tyrone McMillan, who is black, stands accused of killing a white woman and a white man in Stedman in 2006. His lawyer was also in the meeting with the Cumberland County judge to strategize on McMillan's planned use of the Racial Justice Act.

The idea that a victim's race could influence the amount of justice they qualify for . . . is simply outrageous.

The possibilities in McMillan's case are endless because the whole thing is dangerously open to statistical interpretation. He could argue that since he killed a white woman, or man, that he is more likely to get the death penalty and that that is racially unfair. Or he could argue that African-Americans make up 22 percent of North Carolina's population, but 53 percent of inmates on the state's death row, therefore he is being discriminated against. A liberal judge might buy that and commute his death sentence to life in prison. A less liberal judge might buy the prosecutor's rebuttal that blacks make up 62 percent of all convicted murderers in the state's prison system, as the *Winston-Salem Journal* recently theorized, and are actually underrepresented on death row.

Smith might not be down for the count either. He could argue that while they are underrepresented on death row when compared to their numbers in the state population, once convicted of murder, white killers are more likely than black killers to get the death penalty. In 2005, for instance, 38 percent of convicted killers in the state were white, while 39 percent of those on death row were white.

The idea that a victim's race could influence the amount of justice they qualify for, that a couple of these cases could establish a precedent that makes it harder for homicidal maniacs to get the death penalty for killing a white woman in this state, is simply outrageous.

I recently sent an information request to the governor, asking if a lower standard of justice for entire victim classes based on their sex or race was an acceptable outcome from the bill she signed. I got back a non-answer from Perdue that dodged my question.

"The Racial Justice Act was enacted by the General Assembly to assure that no person is discriminated against because of race in application of the death penalty," the statement said. "Certainty the courts may be called upon to interpret this new law, and we are confident they will apply the RJA consistent with the legislature's purpose."

10

Physician Participation in Executions Is Unethical

Daniel N. Lerman

Daniel N. Lerman is a contributing writer for the Georgetown Law Journal.

In order for the death penalty to be constitutional and adhere to the Eighth Amendment's decree against cruel punishment and the unnecessary infliction of pain, state governments have requested the presence of physicians during executions to ensure that anesthesia is properly administered. But physician participation in capital punishment violates medical ethics with regard to the pledge "first do no harm" and the commitment to preserve life. Furthermore, physician involvement in lethal injection erodes a trustful relationship between doctor and patient, and trust in the medical profession as a whole.

On April 21, 2006, Willie Brown, Jr. was executed by lethal injection in North Carolina by officials using a machine—rather than a trained physician—to ensure he did not suffer unconstitutional pain.

In response to mounting evidence that inmates were not properly anesthetized during lethal injections and may therefore have experienced excruciating pain in violation of the Eighth Amendment, U.S. District Judge Malcolm Howard ordered that Brown's execution could proceed only in the presence of "personnel with sufficient medical training to ensure

Daniel N. Lerman, "Second Opinion: Inconsistent Deference to Medical Ethics in Death Penalty Jurisprudence," *Georgetown Law Journal*, Vol. 95, pp. 1941–78, 2007. Reproduced by permission of the author.

that [Brown] is in all respects unconscious prior to and at the time of" the execution. But that order placed the state in a potentially untenable position because medical ethics forbid physicians from participating in executions. Thus, the state devised an execution protocol that used the machine, a bispectral index (BIS) monitor, rather than physicians and nurses, to monitor Brown's level of consciousness. The problem with this strategy was that while the state claimed the machine would ensure that Brown was rendered unconscious during the execution, it was widely accepted by anesthesiologists that the BIS monitor alone is insufficient to monitor anesthetic depth, as the manufacturer of the machine itself stated in its product literature. Indeed, the company's medical director called the sale of the device "a regrettable system failure" and accused the North Carolina Department of Corrections of lying about its intended use in order to obtain the device. Despite these problems, however, Judge Howard accepted the state's proposal to use the monitor during Brown's execution.

The "Dual Loyalty" Problem for Physicians

The use of the BIS monitor during Brown's execution highlights the difficult question of the extent to which courts should defer to medical ethics where physicians are participants in the criminal justice system. Physicians serve a variety of roles in criminal proceedings, from evaluating a defendant's competency to stand trial or be executed, to providing voluntary and involuntary medical treatments to prisoners, to participating in executions of condemned inmates. But who should decide whether such procedures at the intersection of law and clinical practice are acceptable—the legislature, the courts, or the medical profession? Should judicial decisions rely on medical ethics, and if so, when? Recent death penalty jurisprudence suggests that, despite the importance of these questions, the courts have failed to present a coherent answer. In some recent cases, courts have deferred to medical ethics when rendering decisions on the constitutionality of clinical activities that would facilitate an inmate's execution, while in others courts have dismissed or ignored medical ethics. . . .

Virtually every medical and humanitarian organization to address the issue opposes the participation of physicians in capital punishment.

Medical ethicists oppose physician participation in capital punishment on the grounds that such involvement violates physicians' ethical obligation not to harm patients and inappropriately subsumes the interests of the patient to those of the state. Yet doctors are often compelled to serve not just the interests of their patients but also those of society, and the ethical conflict that arises when physicians participate in lethal injections results from this "dual loyalty" problem. Moreover, many state laws allow or even require physician participation in executions, often shielding physicians from liability by providing that such participation does not constitute the practice of medicine and presumably does not trigger the doctors' professional ethical obligations. As a result of these laws, and their underlying denial of ethical obligations, physicians play a variety of roles that facilitate capital punishment, in spite of the widespread ethical consensus prohibiting such involvement. Moreover, in denying that ethical obligations are even implicated, this view that physicians are acting outside of their normal medical role when participating in executions circumvents the question of judicial deference to medical ethics.

A Physician's Dedication to Preserving Life

Virtually every medical and humanitarian organization to address the issue opposes the participation of physicians in capital punishment. For many medical societies and ethicists, this opposition is rooted in the Hippocratic dictum, "first do no harm," as well as the modern professional ideal of nonmaleficence [practicing medicine without ill intentions]. As the American Medical Association's (AMA's) Council on Ethical and Judicial Affairs noted, "[p]hysician participation in executions contradicts the dictates of the medical profession by causing harm rather than alleviating pain and suffering." Accordingly, the AMA's Code of Medical Ethics states that "[a] physician, as a member of a profession dedicated to preserving life where there is hope of doing so, should not be a participant in a legally authorized execution." Many other medical societies have also adopted policies prohibiting physician participation in execution, including the American College of Physicians (ACP), American Psychiatric Association (APA), World Medical Association, American Nurses Association, and the Society of Correctional Physicians, and more than half of state medical associations have also spoken against physician participation in executions. The AMA Code also explicitly forbids physicians from treating a condemned prisoner for the purposes of restoring his competency to be executed, unless a commutation is granted prior to the commencement of treatment.

Physician involvement in lethal injection erodes the public's trust in the medical profession as a whole.

Opponents of physician participation in execution also argue that such participation will erode the public trust in the medical profession. This breach of trust can occur at various levels, ranging from the individual patient to society at large. At the individual level, trust is essential to the doctor-patient relationship. While one could reasonably argue that no such relationship exists between a doctor and the inmate she is helping to execute, or that trust is not essential in this context, concerns over an erosion of trust are heightened when a physician forcibly medicates an inmate to render him competent to be executed. Such involuntary medication prevents a trustful relationship between the physician and her patient and therefore inhibits the efficacy of any subsequent treatment of that patient's mental illness. Further, participation in either lethal injection or involuntary medication can compromise a doctor's relationship with the entire inmate population, thereby interfering with effective treatment of this class of patients. Finally, physician involvement in lethal injection erodes the public's trust in the medical profession as a whole. Society trusts that physicians work to heal, not harm, their patients, and this trust is threatened by physician involvement in lethal injection or in medicating to restore competency for execution. [According to Jonathan I. Groner,] "When doctors enter the death chamber, they harm not only their relationship with their own patients but the relationships of all doctors with their patients."

Supporters of physician participation in lethal injection respond that physicians are obligated to relieve suffering, and it is thus in the patient's best interest that trained physicians be involved with starting intravenous lines and measuring and administering drugs to ensure that the execution proceeds as quickly and painlessly as possible. The patient here has no hope—like a terminally ill patient, his death is unavoidable, and failure of a doctor to participate would actually cause the patient more pain. However, this argument fails for several reasons. First, while a physician may wish to comfort a condemned inmate, strictly speaking the inmate is not her patient. The inmate cannot refuse the physician's care, nor is he or his family permitted to know the doctor's identity. Second, physician participation gives lethal injection the veneer of humanity: it sanitizes the perception of the procedure by the public, and gives it an "aura of medical legitimacy." Support for lethal injection over other execution methods derives in large part from this medicalization: it mimics anesthesia techniques, uses known drugs, and relies on the technical expertise of physicians, contributing to society's perception of a professionally-administered and humane method of execution. Indeed, "without the respectability that lethal injection provides, capital punishment in the United States would probably cease." Widespread accounts of botched executions lend urgency to calls for increased physician participation in and oversight of lethal injections. Third, the very constitutionality of lethal injection may depend on physician participation. Thus, it is misleading to suggest that physicians who participate in lethal injections are merely comforting a "terminally ill" patient who would otherwise die; in many respects, such physicians are a but-for cause of the execution. Without their involvement, the procedure would not enjoy such widespread societal—and perhaps even legal—support.

Supporters of physician participation in executions also suggest that opponents overstate the resultant erosion in trust in the medical profession. Kenneth Baum, for example, argues that just as the presence of priests at executions does not destroy the public's trust in the church, a doctor's involvement in executions will not erode the public's trust in physicians. However, this analogy is inappropriate because physicians participate more directly in executions than do priests. Further, the Supreme Court has argued that physician participation in assisted suicide could "undermine the trust that is essential to the doctor-patient relationship by blurring the time-honored line between healing and harming." If assisting a patient who *wants* to die will undermine trust, then so too would participating in the execution of an inmate who wants to live. . . .

Physicians as "Non-Doctors"

The chief obstacle to initiating disciplinary proceedings against physician participants in lethal injection is the enactment of legislation providing that participation in lethal injection does not constitute the practice of medicine. Several states have enacted such laws, which effectively shield doctors who participate in lethal injection from disciplinary actions by state medical boards. For example, Florida law provides that "prescription, preparation, compounding, dispensing, and administration of a lethal injection does not constitute the practice of medicine, nursing, or pharmacy." In addition to providing safe harbor for doctors who breach medical ethics by participating in executions, these laws essentially declare that such physicians are "non-doctors" when participating in executions. That is, a doctor is defined not by her actions, but rather by what hat she is wearing when she commits such actions. This assertion that lethal injection is not the practice of medicine is analogous to Appelbaum's argument that the application of psychiatric expertise in a legal context is not the practice of psychiatry, and similarly results in a dismissal of the relevance of medical ethics. As a result of such safe harbor provisions, none of the physicians who have faced challenges for violating professional ethics by participating in lethal injections have lost their licenses as a result. Further, even in the absence of statutes specifically providing legal immunity to physicians for participating in executions, courts have rejected claims that such participation constitutes unethical or unprofessional conduct.

Yet the notion that a physician who participates in lethal injection is not practicing medicine is particularly absurd in light of the doctor's extensive involvement in the procedure. Rather than defining medical practice according to whether the physician is serving the clinical interests of a patient versus the extraclinical interests of a third party, the practice of medicine should be defined as any practice in which a physician uses her clinical skills and training. This skills-based rather than role-based definition would go a long way toward resolving disputes over when ethical duties attach to a physician's activities. For example, under this definition, a military doctor's participation in torture would implicate (and violate) professional ethics, but a military doctor who happens to be a bomber pilot would not violate medical ethics when bombing human targets, because in the latter case the pilot is not using his clinical skills to do harm, whereas in the former case the physician is relying on his medical skills to harm the subject. Further confusing the issue, however, some opponents of physician participation in executions also suggest that lethal injection is not the practice of medicine in order to highlight the impropriety of such participation.

Thus, while medical ethicists and professional societies are nearly unanimous in their opposition to physician participation in capital punishment, supporters of such participation attempt to circumvent this problem by characterizing physicians who participate in capital punishment as non-doctors serving the societal goal of justice. But this approach only serves as an end-run around the debate over judicial deference to medical ethics. That is, if we accept that a physician is not acting as a doctor when serving the interests of the criminal justice system, then we need not confront the question of whether a court should defer to medical ethics—because such ethical obligations are not implicated in the first place. Courts allowing physician participation in capital proceedings appear to endorse this approach in asserting that no ethical obligations are implicated by physician involvement in capital punishment. On the other hand, courts that do defer to medical ethics squarely address the ethical implications of physician participation in executions.

11

Physician Participation in Executions Is Not Unethical

Dudley Sharp

Dudley Sharp, a published author, has written extensively on the subject of capital punishment and has appeared on national television and radio stations.

Some professionals in the medical community cite the Hippocratic Oath with its "do no harm" principle as grounds for prohibiting physician involvement in state executions. Neither the classical version nor the modern version of the Hippocratic Oath, however, makes any reference to the execution of murderers. In fact, there is a distinct separation between the criminal justice system and the medical profession; one has nothing to do with the other ethically or morally. Therefore, there is no foundation for the claim that physician participation in executions is unethical.

Some in the medical community have attempted to create an ethical prohibition against medical professionals' involvement in state executions by invoking the famous "do no harm" credo and the Hippocratic Oath.

It is a dishonest effort. Neither reference is in the context of the state execution of murderers. I find the effort to ban medical professionals' participation in executions an unethical effort to fabricate professional ethical standards, based upon personal anti-death penalty feelings.

Dudley Sharp, "Physicians and the State Execution of Murderers: No Ethical/Medical Dilemma," HomicideSurvivors.com, October 24, 2009. Copyright © 2009 by Dudley Sharp. Reproduced by permission of the author.

The Hippocratic Oath—Classical Version

The select Hippocratic Oath quote in its original (translated) form is: "I will neither give a deadly drug to anybody who asked for it, nor will I make a suggestion to this effect. Similarly I will not give to a woman an abortive remedy. In purity and holiness I will guard my life and my art."

This is a prohibition against euthanasia and abortion and has nothing to do with the fabricated medical prohibition of participation in state-sanctioned executions.

I am unaware of any other ancient texts or translations which indicate a historical context, with that quote, that prohibits physicians from participation in executions.

In 2004, Dr. [Howard] Markel, a medical historian, writes, "There are two highly controversial vows in the original Hippocratic Oath that we continue to ponder and struggle with as a profession: the pledges never to participate in euthanasia and abortion."

In reality, these are barely controversial, now. They are, however, inconvenient. Dr. Markel's article never mentions a context of state execution of murderers, because the oath has nothing to do with it.

Dr. Markel continues: "The Hippocratics' reasons for refusing to participate in euthanasia may have been based on a philosophical or moral belief in preserving the sanctity of life or simply on their wish to avoid involvement in any act of assisted suicide, murder, or manslaughter."

Dr. Markel is speculating. What we do know is that it was a reference to euthanasia and abortion, specifically. There is not even speculation by Dr. Markel that the reference had anything to do with the state execution of murderers.

The following are "... the results of a study ... in which 157 deans of allopathic and osteopathic schools of medicine in Canada and the United States were surveyed regarding the use of the Hippocratic Oath":

1. In 1993, 98% schools administered some form of the Oath.

2. In 1928, only 26% of schools administered some form of the Oath.

3. Only 1 school used the original Hippocratic Oath.

4. 68 schools used versions of the original Hippocratic Oath.

5. 100% of current Oaths pledge a commitment to patients.

6. Only 43% vow to be accountable for their actions.

7. 14% include a prohibition against euthanasia.

8. Only 11% invoke a diety.

9. 8% prohibit abortion.

10. Only 3% prohibit sexual contact with patients.

There is no mention of the state execution of murderers, because the Hippocratic Oath has nothing to do with it.

Although there is no prohibition on the death penalty, there is one against both euthanasia and abortion. Yet, various medical associations have fabricated an imagined ethical problem with the death penalty and have, nearly, fully accepted both abortion and euthanasia.

Now, only 3% prohibit sexual contact with patients, but the original Hippocratic Oath states: "Whatever houses I may visit, I will come for the benefit of the sick, remaining free of all intentional injustice, of all mischief and in particular of sexual relations with both female and male persons, be they free or slaves."

100% pledge a commitment to their patients, but only 43% vow being accountable for their medical actions. Some commitment. What ethics?

With these survey results and with medical professionals bringing up the Hippocratic Oath as if it has something to say in the death penalty debate, possibly we should, now, in the true context of euthanasia and abortion and other issues, call it what it has become, the Hypocrisy Oath.

For example, in January 2007, the North Carolina Medical Board adopted a policy that physicians participating in executions may lose their licence. In 2009, the North Carolina Supreme Court vacated the Board's policy, finding that they had exceeded their authority.

Did the Board attempt to prevent physicians from performing abortions, or have they issued a statement condemning physicians' participation in euthanasia? Of course not.

The Oath of Hippocrates—Modern Version

The modern version is most often identified as that penned by Louis Lasagna in 1964.

It states: "It may also be within my power to take a life; this awesome responsibility must be faced with great humbleness and awareness of my own frailty."

This is in the context of killing innocent lives through either abortion or euthanasia. Quite the about-face. The quote shows physicians' medical ethical/moral acceptance of taking innocent lives.

Executions do not make death row inmates patients.

[Dr. Howard Markel wrote in a 2004 *New England Journal of Medicine* article] "The famous physician credo 'First, do no harm' (a phrase translated into Latin as *Primum non nocere*) is often mistakenly ascribed to the (Hippocratic) oath, although it appears nowhere in that venerable pledge. Hippocrates came closest to issuing this directive in his treatise *Epidemics*, in an axiom that reads, 'As to disease, make a habit of two things—to help, or at least, to do no harm.'"

"As to disease" [Hippocrates wrote]. Nothing else. There is no relevance outside medicine and most certainly no prohibition against medical professionals' participation in the state execution of murderers.

Criminal Justice—Not Medical Treatment

Those ethical codes pertain to the medical profession, only, and to patients, only.

Judicial execution is not part of the medical profession and executions do not make death row inmates patients. Is that news?

The editors of the *Public Library of Science* (PLoS) agree. They write: "Execution by lethal injection, even if it uses tools of intensive care such as intravenous tubing and beeping heart monitors, has the same relationship to medicine that an executioner's axe has to surgery."

So too, the American Society of Anesthesiologists: "Although lethal injection mimics certain technical aspects of the practice of anesthesia, capital punishment in any form is not the practice of medicine."

Both confirm the obvious point: The state execution of murderers is not equivalent or connected to the medical treatment of patients. There is no ethical or moral connection. Hardly a mystery. Any rational person can see that the state execution of murderers is not a medical treatment, but a criminal justice sanction. The basis for medical treatment is to improve the plight of the patient, for which the medical profession provides obvious and daily exceptions. The basis for execution is to carry out a criminal justice sentence where death is the sanction.

Doctors and nurses can be police and soldiers and can kill, when deemed appropriate, within those lines of duty and without violating the ethical codes of their medical profession, because there is no ethical connection. Similarly, medical professionals do not violate medical codes of ethics when participating in the state execution of murderers.

Appropriate "Do No Harm" Exceptions

Physicians are often part of double or triple blind studies where there is hope that the tested drugs may, someday, prove beneficial. The physicians and other researchers know that many patients taking placebos or less effective drugs will suffer more additional harm or death because they are not taking the subject drug or that the subject drug will actually harm or kill more patients than the placebo of other drugs used in the study.

Physicians knowingly harm individual patients, in direct contradiction to their "do no harm" oath. For the greater good, those physicians sacrifice innocent, willing and brave patients. Of course, there have been medical experiments without consent, and even today they continue. Physicians knowingly make exceptions to their "do no harm" requirement every day within their profession where that code actually does apply. And in many cases, they should. There are obvious ethical nuances, and we should consider and pay attention to them as is done within the medical profession.

Physicians and medical institutions should chose ethical guidelines which are truly relevant to their profession.

Many medical professionals need to stop the ridiculous ethical posturing and tell the truth—they don't like the death penalty. In medical writings, against executions, you can easily find a strong bias, evidenced by use of the common and inaccurate anti-death penalty claims, with no apparent effort at fact checking or balance.

Any participation in executions by medical professionals should be a matter for their own personal conscience. In fact, 20–40% of doctors surveyed would participate in the execution process.

If this physician-created mess had been about long-standing medical ethics based upon Hippocrates or "do no harm", then there would be an effort to stop medical professionals from participating in euthanasia and abortion. In fact, the opposite has occurred. Instead, irresponsible medical professionals have turned those obvious, historical ethical standards upside down and have fabricated out of thin air a prohibition against the death penalty.

Why? For personal reasons, some have decided the formerly unethical medical practices of abortion and euthanasia are now just fine and that the non-medical death penalty is prohibited by a fabricated medical ethic.

There is no foundation for an ethical prohibition against medical professionals participating in executions. Stop using personal bias to fabricate one.

It's unethical.

12

The Death Penalty Violates Human Rights

Amnesty International

Founded in London in 1961, Amnesty International is a grass-roots activist organization that focuses on preventing and ending abuses of human rights worldwide.

Every human being has certain basic human rights, the most fundamental of which is the right to life. The death penalty, however, brings into question whether a government has the authority to deprive a person of this fundamental right to life. The particular justifications given for advocating the death penalty differ from time to time and government to government, and when such an arbitrary and fallible justice system renders a decision as final and irrevocable as the taking of human life, the whole society and its citizens are diminished.

The time has come to abolish the death penalty worldwide. The case for abolition becomes more compelling with each passing year. Everywhere experience shows that executions brutalize those involved in the process. Nowhere has it been shown that the death penalty has any special power to reduce crime or political violence. In country after country, it is used disproportionately against the poor or against racial or ethnic minorities. It is also used as a tool of political repression. It is imposed and inflicted arbitrarily. It is an irrevocable punishment, resulting inevitably in the execution of people innocent of any crime. It is a violation of fundamental human rights.

Over the past decade an average of at least three countries a year have abolished the death penalty, affirming respect for human life and dignity. Yet too many governments still believe that they can solve urgent social or political problems by executing a few or even hundreds of their prisoners. Too many citizens in too many countries are still unaware that the death penalty offers society not further protection but further brutalization. Abolition is gaining ground, but not fast enough.

The death penalty, carried out in the name of the nation's entire population, involves everyone. Everyone should be aware of what the death penalty is, how it is used, how it affects them, how it violates fundamental rights.

The death penalty is the premeditated and cold-blooded killing of a human being by the state. The state can exercise no greater power over a person than that of deliberately depriving him or her of life. At the heart of the case for abolition, therefore, is the question of whether the state has the right to do so.

The death penalty cannot be separated from the issue of human rights.

The Universal Declaration of Human Rights

When the world's nations came together six decades ago to found the United Nations (UN), few reminders were needed of what could happen when a state believed that there was no limit to what it might do to a human being. The staggering extent of state brutality and terror during World War II and the consequences for people throughout the world were still unfolding in December 1948, when the UN General Assembly adopted without dissent the Universal Declaration of Human Rights.

The Universal Declaration is a pledge among nations to promote fundamental rights as the foundation of freedom, justice and peace. The rights it proclaims are inherent in every human being. They are not privileges that may be granted by governments for good behaviour and they may not be withdrawn for bad behaviour. Fundamental human rights limit what a state may do to a man, woman or child.

No matter what reason a government gives for executing prisoners and what method of execution is used, the death penalty cannot be separated from the issue of human rights. The movement for abolition cannot be separated from the movement for human rights.

The Universal Declaration recognizes each person's right to life and categorically states further that "No one shall be subjected to torture or to cruel, inhuman or degrading treatment or punishment." In Amnesty International's view the death penalty violates these rights.

Self-defence may be held to justify, in some cases, the taking of life by state officials: for example, when a country is locked in warfare (international or civil) or when law-enforcement officials must act immediately to save their own lives or those of others. Even in such situations the use of lethal force is surrounded by internationally accepted legal safeguards to inhibit abuse. This use of force is aimed at countering the immediate damage resulting from force used by others.

The death penalty, however, is not an act of self-defence against an immediate threat to life. It is the premeditated killing of a prisoner who could be dealt with equally well by less harsh means.

There can never be a justification for torture or for cruel, inhumane or degrading treatment or punishment. The cruelty of the death penalty is evident. Like torture, an execution constitutes an extreme physical and mental assault on a person already rendered helpless by government authorities.

If hanging a woman by her arms until she experiences excruciating pain is rightly condemned as torture, how does one describe hanging her by the neck until she is dead? If administering 100 volts of electricity to the most sensitive parts of a man's body evokes disgust, what is the appropriate reaction to the administration of 2,000 volts to his body in order to kill him? If a pistol held to the head or a chemical substance injected to cause protracted suffering are clearly instruments of torture, how should they be identified when used to kill by shooting or lethal injection? Does the use of legal process in these cruelties make their inhumanity justifiable?. . .

No Contribution to the "Greater Good"

The particular needs claimed to be served by the death penalty differ from time to time and from society to society. In some countries the penalty is considered legitimate as a means of preventing or punishing the crime of murder. Elsewhere it may be deemed indispensable to stop drug-trafficking, acts of political terror, economic corruption or adultery. In yet other countries, it is used to eliminate those seen as posing a political threat to the authorities.

Once one state uses the death penalty for any reason, it becomes easier for other states to use it with an appearance of legitimacy for whatever reasons they may choose. If the death penalty can be justified for one offence, justifications that accord with the prevailing view of a society or its rulers will be found for it to be used for other offences. Whatever purpose is cited, the idea that a government can justify a punishment as cruel as death conflicts with the very concept of human rights. The significance of human rights is precisely that some means may never be used to protect society because their use violates the very values which make society worth protecting. When this essential distinction between appropriate and inappropriate means is set aside in the name of some "greater good," all rights are vulnerable and all individuals are threatened.

The death penalty, as a violation of fundamental human rights, would be wrong even if it could be shown that it uniquely met a vital social need. What makes the use of the death penalty even more indefensible and the case for its abolition even more compelling is that it has never been shown to have any special power to meet any genuine social need.

Countless men and women have been executed for the stated purpose of preventing crime, especially the crime of murder. Yet Amnesty International has failed to find convincing evidence that the death penalty has any unique capacity to deter others from committing particular crimes. A survey of research findings on the relation between the death penalty and homicide rates, conducted for the UN in 1988 and updated in 2002, concluded: ". . . it is not prudent to accept the hypothesis that capital punishment deters murder to a marginally greater extent than does the threat and application of the supposedly lesser punishment of life imprisonment."

Human rights apply to the worst of us as well as to the best of us, which is why they protect all of us.

Undeniably the death penalty, by permanently "incapacitating" a prisoner, prevents that person from repeating the crime. But there is no way to be sure that the prisoner would indeed have repeated the crime if allowed to live, nor is there any need to violate the prisoner's right to life for the purpose of incapacitation: dangerous offenders can be kept safely away from the public without resorting to execution, as shown by the experience of many abolitionist countries.

Nor is there evidence that the threat of the death penalty will prevent politically motivated crimes or acts of terror. If anything, the possibility of political martyrdom through execution may encourage people to commit such crimes.

Every society seeks protection from crimes. Far from being a solution, the death penalty gives the erroneous impression that "firm measures" are being taken against crime. It diverts attention from the more complex measures which are really needed. In the words of the South African Constitution Court in 1995, "We would be deluding ourselves if we were to believe that the execution of . . . a comparatively few people each year . . . will provide the solution to the unacceptably high rate of crime. . . . The greatest deterrent to crime is the likelihood that offenders will be apprehended, convicted and punished."

Vengeance Disguised as Retribution

When the arguments of deterrence and incapacitation fall away, one is left with a more deep-seated justification for the death penalty: that of just retribution for the particular crime committed. According to this argument, certain people deserve to be killed as repayment for the evil done: there are crimes so offensive that killing the offender is the only just response.

It is an emotionally powerful argument. It is also one which, if valid, would invalidate the basis for human rights. If a person who commits a terrible act can "deserve" the cruelty of death, why cannot others, for similar reasons, "deserve" to be tortured or imprisoned without trial or simply shot on sight? Central to fundamental human rights is that they are inalienable. They may not be taken away even if a person has committed the most atrocious of crimes. Human rights apply to the worst of us as well as to the best of us, which is why they protect all of us.

What the argument for retribution boils down to is often no more than a desire for vengeance masked as a principle of justice. The desire for vengeance can be understood and acknowledged but the exercise of vengeance must be resisted. The history of the endeavour to establish the rule of law is a history of the progressive restriction of personal vengeance in public policy and legal codes.

If today's penal systems do not sanction the burning of an arsonist's home, the rape of the rapist or the torture of the torturer, it is not because they tolerate the crimes. Instead, it is because societies understand that they must be built on a different set of values from those they condemn.

An execution cannot be used to condemn killing; it is killing. Such an act by the state is the mirror image of the criminal's willingness to use physical violence against a victim.

Related to the argument that some people "deserve" to die is the proposition that the state is capable of determining exactly who they are. Whatever one's view of the retribution argument may be, the practice of the death penalty reveals that no criminal justice system is, or conceivably could be, capable of deciding fairly, consistently and infallibly who should live and who should die.

Arbitrary Judgments

All criminal justice systems are vulnerable to discrimination and error. Expediency, discretionary decisions and prevailing public opinion may influence the proceedings at every stage from the initial arrest to the last-minute decision clemency. The reality of the death penalty is that what determines who shall be executed and who shall be spared is often not only the nature of the crimes but also the ethnic and social background, the financial means or the political opinions of the defendant. The death penalty is used disproportionately against the poor, the powerless, the marginalised or those whom repressive governments deem it expedient to eliminate.

Human uncertainty and arbitrary judgements are factors which affect all judicial decisions. But only one decision—the decision to execute—results in something that cannot be remedied or undone. Whether executions take place within hours of a summary trial or after years of protracted legal proceedings, states will continue to execute people who are later found to be innocent. Those executed cannot be compensated for loss of life and the whole society must share responsibility for what has been done.

It is the irrevocable nature of the death penalty, the fact that the prisoner is eliminated forever, that makes the penalty so tempting to some states as a tool of repression. Thousands have been put to death under one government only to be recognized as innocent victims when another set of authorities comes to power. Only abolition can ensure that such political abuse of the death penalty will never occur.

When used to crush political dissent, the death penalty is abhorrent. When invoked as a way to protect society from crime, it is illusory. Wherever used, it brutalizes those involved in the process and conveys to the public a sense that killing a defenceless prisoner is somehow acceptable. It may be used to try to bolster the authority of the state—or of those who govern in its name. But any such authority it confers is spurious. The penalty is a symbol of terror and, to that extent, a confession of weakness. It is always a violation of the most fundamental human rights.

Each society and its citizens have the choice to decide about the sort of world people want and will work to achieve: a world in which the state is permitted to kill as a legal punishment or a world based on respect for human life and human rights—a world without executions.

13

The Death Penalty Should Be Decided Only Under a Specific Guideline

Louis Klarevas

Louis Klarevas, a professor at New York University's Center for Global Affairs, has written several articles and commentaries regarding such issues as international security, transnational terrorism, American foreign policy, and national security law.

A dilemma inherent to the death penalty is the need to fittingly punish a murderer without ever executing an innocent person. Because it is impossible to make reparations or undo the damage caused by a wrongful execution, the standards for sentencing a person to death must be set higher than for any other legal action. The principle for jurors of "beyond a reasonable doubt" is a just application when determining guilt or innocence, but it is not enough of a safeguard when determining a sentence of death. For that ultimate punishment, there should be absolutely no doubt whatsoever.

Barring an eleventh hour intervention by the governor of Virginia, the D.C. sniper John Muhammad will be put to death for his role in the shooting spree that claimed 10 lives and terrorized the nation's capital in 2002.

Tomorrow's [November 10, 2009] execution sets the stage for the story I want to share about a dinner I had recently with a good friend.

My friend, an American diplomat, had been at the United Nations in New York a few weeks ago, discussing, among other things, the death penalty with European Union colleagues. Coincidentally, that same week a controversy was brewing in Texas over Gov. Rick Perry's decision to replace three members of the State Forensic Science Commission just as the commission was about to investigate whether Texas had executed an innocent man in 2004.

Incensed by the idea that innocent people might have been put to death for crimes they did not commit—and no doubt primed by his European counterparts—my friend made a passionate argument for why the death penalty should be abolished in the U.S.

Knowing his personal connection to a capital crime, I couldn't resist asking, "And you would support such a ban even if it meant that the D.C. sniper would be spared?"

His friend being one of Muhammad's 10 victims, he fell momentarily silent before finally conceding, "No, he deserves to die."

A Fear of Executing the Innocent

And therein lies the dilemma we face as a nation when it comes to capital punishment: No one wants to see an innocent person put to death—but some criminals deserve to die for their offenses.

This dilemma is reflected in two conflicting views on the death penalty that permeate American society. On the one hand, our awareness of flaws with capital punishment is increasing as result of technological advances. According to the Death Penalty Information Center, there have been nearly 1,200 executions in the past 25 years. This may not shock too many people. But what is shocking is that, in the same time period, there have been nearly 140 exonerations of death row inmates. That's over 10%! Just as interesting, the average number of releases from death row between 1973 and 1999 was 3 per year. With the increased introduction of exculpatory DNA evidence, this number has risen to 5 per year in the past decade.

The conclusion is inescapable: innocent people are often sentenced to death.

On the other hand, our desire for eye-for-an-eye justice against those who murder our fellow citizens also increases when the media bombard us with real-time coverage of acts of violence. Continuous footage of the Oklahoma City bombings, the D.C. sniper spree, the Fort Hood rampage, and similar events leaves us feeling victimized and angry. The consequence is a need to punish those responsible for these heinous crimes with the ultimate sanction: death.

The standard for depriving life is no different than the standard for depriving the lesser right of liberty.

As we wrestle with how to continue punishing the truly guilty while better protecting the truly innocent, let me suggest a compromise measure which, although still imperfect, will go further in safeguarding against misapplications of the death penalty.

In the United States, we are all entitled to "life, liberty, and the pursuit of happiness." However, these "rights," if you can call them that, are not equal. While we should all enjoy happiness, government cannot—and need not—go far out of its way to help us pursue it.

Liberty is a different story. There is a high legal standard that must be overcome before someone can be imprisoned. The deprivation of liberty requires that the accused first be found guilty, beyond a reasonable doubt, of committing a crime.

In theory, the right to life is the strongest right any American possesses. The standard for depriving one of life should be higher than any other legal action. In practice, though, this is not the case. The standard for depriving life is no different than the standard for depriving the lesser right of liberty: conviction based on evidence that establishes guilt beyond a reasonable doubt.

Prior to being able to impose the death penalty, the jury must conclude that the accused is guilty beyond any doubt.

As anyone who has watched a crime drama knows, beyond a reasonable doubt does not mean beyond a shadow of a doubt. The existence of doubt as to guilt is not enough for a juror to avoid a finding of guilty. So long as a juror feels that the prosecution has established guilt beyond a reasonable doubt, that juror is obligated to vote guilty. Unfortunately, the system is far from perfect and, from time-to-time, juries are wrong.

The largest (and most obvious) problem is that, while someone wrongfully convicted can always be released (and compensated for damages), once someone is deprived of life by the state, there is no way to undo the damage. Therefore, we must do everything we can to assure that this right—the most important right to which all Americans are entitled—is safeguarded from erroneous deprivation. As the late Supreme Court Justice Harry Blackmun once declared, "Nothing could be more contrary to contemporary standards of decency or shocking to the conscience than to execute a person who is actually innocent."

To reduce the likelihood of a miscarriage of justice, let me propose a bifurcated standard for capital cases—one for the trial phase and one for the sentencing phase. I believe that juries should continue applying the beyond a reasonable doubt standard for determinations of guilt in capital cases (which speaks to deprivations of liberty), but the standard for sentencing someone to death (which speaks to deprivations of life) must be elevated to a stricter standard: beyond a lingering doubt.

As the Constitution Project argued in a 2005 report of death penalty reform: "Given the irrevocable nature of the penalty of death, a decision to impose the penalty requires a greater degree of reliability than is required for imposition of other penalties. Jurors should not vote for the death penalty if they entertain doubts as to the defendant's factual guilt."

In other words, after a jury finds someone guilty of a capital crime but prior to being able to impose the death penalty, the jury must conclude that the accused is guilty beyond *any* doubt. As a society, our own lingering doubts on the effectiveness of the current capital punishment system leave us with no other conclusion.

14

Capital Punishment Is Too Expensive to Retain

Richard C. Dieter

Richard C. Dieter is the Executive Director of the Death Penalty Information Center, a nonprofit organization that provides analysis and information on issues concerning capital punishment.

In the last several decades, the US death penalty has proven to be an expensive and wasteful government program that consumes valuable resources. In fact, the majority of police chiefs and criminologists nationwide believe the death penalty is the least effective tool for reducing crime, and that the millions of dollars spent on court and prison costs inherent in death penalty cases would be much better utilized by hiring additional police officers, improving forensic labs and DNA testing, and providing drug treatment and crime-prevention programs.

The death penalty in the U.S. is an enormously expensive and wasteful program with no clear benefits. All of the studies on the cost of capital punishment conclude it is much more expensive than a system with life sentences as the maximum penalty. In a time of painful budget cutbacks, states are pouring money into a system that results in a declining number of death sentences and executions that are almost exclusively carried out in just one area of the country. As many states face further deficits, it is an appropriate time to consider whether maintaining the costly death penalty system is being smart on crime.

The nation's police chiefs rank the death penalty last in their priorities for effective crime reduction. The officers do not believe the death penalty acts as a deterrent to murder, and they rate it as one of most inefficient uses of taxpayer dollars in fighting crime. Criminologists concur that the death penalty does not effectively reduce the number of murders.

Around the country, death sentences have declined 60% since 2000 and executions have declined almost as much. Yet maintaining a system with 3,300 people on death row and supporting new prosecutions for death sentences that likely will never be carried out is becoming increasingly expensive and harder to justify. The money spent to preserve this failing system could be directed to effective programs that make society safer. . . .

Police Reject Deterrence Theory

A significant reason why police chiefs do not favor use of the death penalty is that they do not believe it deters murders. Only 37% of those polled believed the death penalty significantly reduces the number of homicides. Fifty-seven percent (57%) agreed: "The death penalty does little to prevent violent crimes because perpetrators rarely consider the consequences when engaged in violence." Only 24% of the respondents believe murderers think about the range of possible punishments before committing homicides.

The leading criminologists in the country agree with the police chiefs about deterrence. A recent [2009] survey showed that 88% of the country's top criminologists do not believe the death penalty acts as a deterrent to homicide.

Eighty-seven percent (87%) believe abolition of the death penalty would have no significant effect on murder rates. The authors concluded:

> Our survey indicates that the vast majority of the world's top criminologists believe that the empirical research has re-

vealed the deterrence hypothesis for a myth ... [T]he consensus among criminologists is that the death penalty does not add any significant deterrent effect above that of long-term imprisonment.

Over many years, deterrence studies have been inconclusive, with most experts concluding that the relative rarity of executions and their concentration in a few states renders national conclusions about a deterrent effect to the death penalty unreliable. If the goal is to deter homicides, the police chiefs have pointed to many ways of achieving it far more effectively than the death penalty.

Money Better Spent Elsewhere

On the state and federal level, efforts are being made to eliminate government programs that do not work and to address deficits through layoffs, shorter hours for governmental services, and higher fees. But so far the death penalty has largely escaped the budgetary scalpel. Capital punishment uses enormous resources on a few cases, with little to show for it. This was the principal reason Colorado's legislature came within one vote this year [2009] of passing a bill to abolish the death penalty and use the money saved to deal with unsolved cases, as victims' families had requested.

The money saved by giving up the death penalty is desperately needed elsewhere.

The same states that are spending millions of dollars on the death penalty are facing severe cutbacks in other justice areas. Courts are open less, trials are delayed, and even police are being furloughed.

- In Florida, the courts have lost 10% of their funding, with another cut expected, as home foreclosures accelerated.

- Philadelphia is leaving 200 police positions unfilled.

- Police in Atlanta had a 10% pay cut through a furlough of 4 hours per week, even as the region experienced an increase in crime.

- In New Hampshire, civil and criminal jury trials were halted for a month to save money; in one county, 77 criminal trials were delayed for up to six months.

- Public defenders in Kentucky, Tennessee, and Florida are overburdened with caseloads of 400 felonies a year even though national standards set a limit of 150.

- Legal service organizations that provide help to indigent clients in civil matters depend on income from interest rates that are tied to the Federal Reserve's benchmark interest rate. When that rate fell nearly to zero, many legal service organizations were forced to cut staff 20%, just when their services were most needed.

- The legal service agency in East Texas where thousands of people lost their homes in Hurricane Ike in 2008 experienced a budget drop from $16 million to $4 million.

- A recent poll by the Police Executive Research Forum found that 39% of responding police departments said their operating budgets were being cut because of the economy, and 43% said the faltering economy had affected their ability to deliver services.

Clearly, eliminating the death penalty cannot solve all of these problems, but the savings would be significant. Where studies have been done, the excess expenditures *per year* for the death penalty typically are close to $10 million per state. If a new police officer (or teacher, or ambulance driver) is paid

$40,000 per year, this death penalty money could be used to fund 250 additional workers in each state to secure a better community. . . .

Costs alone may not carry the day in deciding the future of an institution as entrenched as capital punishment. The costs of the death penalty must be compared to other ways of achieving a safer community. The money saved by giving up the death penalty is desperately needed elsewhere: for hiring and training police, solving more crimes, improving forensic labs and timely DNA testing, and crime prevention.

The High Cost of Capital Punishment

Every stage of a capital case is more time-consuming and expensive than in a typical criminal case. If the defendant is found guilty of a capital crime, an entire separate trial is required, with new witnesses and new evidence, in which the jury must decide whether the penalty should be death or life imprisonment without the possibility of parole. Two attorneys are often appointed for the defense, so that issues of guilt and sentencing can be separately explored. The prosecution has to respond with equal or greater resources since they have the burden of proof.

Experts are needed to examine the forensic evidence and to explore the mental health of the defendant. For every expert on one side, the other side needs a rebuttal. In a thoroughly defended case, mitigating and aggravating evidence is compiled and examined. Mitigation experts must probe aspects of the defendant's life from birth to the present. Relatives, co-workers, supervisors, teachers, and doctors are interviewed. The state matches this testimony with evidence of aggravating factors and expert testimony denigrating the defendant's past.

The mental health of the defendant at the time of the crime may become a major issue, with psychiatrists called to testify. If a defendant is mentally retarded, he cannot receive the death penalty, though that determination alone can result in considerable expense. If at any time he was mentally ill, that will be a mitigating factor to be presented to the jury. Most of the preparation for this presentation must be done in advance, whether or not a sentencing trial actually turns out to be necessary. (Of course, in states that are not so thorough, the costs will come later when verdicts are overturned and trials have to be done over.)

Jury selection in a capital case can take weeks or even months. Each person's position on the death penalty is explored in detail by the judge, the prosecutor and defense attorney. Such questioning about the eventual punishment of the defendant would not be allowed in a non-death penalty case, and it makes jury selection take much longer in capital cases. Potential jurors must be carefully questioned about their willingness to vote for the death penalty or life imprisonment; any prospective juror who cannot fairly consider both sentencing alternatives is excluded from serving.

Jurors may also be struck for no stated reason. Although race and gender are improper considerations in selecting a jury, they are statistically related to people's views on the death penalty. Hence, jury selection can involve lengthy disputes about whether a particular juror was struck legitimately because of her doubts about the death penalty or unfairly because of her race. With regard to costs, the end result is that jury selection costs much more in capital cases because it takes much longer.

Death penalty trials often conclude with no death sentence. The defendant may be acquitted or sentenced to prison. However, the process of getting to that point is much more expensive because the case was prosecuted as a capital case. If a death sentence is imposed, there are mandatory appeals. Unlike in ordinary criminal cases where the main focus of an appeal is the conviction, capital defendants are entitled to full review of their death sentence as well. A reversal can mean a new sentencing trial with another jury, more witnesses, and another chance that no death sentence will be imposed. Additional appeals may look at constitutional challenges, such as the effectiveness of defense counsel or the withholding of any evidence that should have been turned over before trial. The entire appeal process can take 15 or 20 years before an execution. The average time between sentencing and execution in 2007 was 12.7 years, the longest of any year since the death penalty was reinstated. In 2006, over 400 inmates around the country had been on death row for 20 years or more, with some cases going back to 1974. Despite the length of this process, however, it is the pre-trial and trial costs that make up the majority of death penalty expenses, not the appeal.

The time that inmates spend on death row also adds to the costs of the death penalty because of the extra security required compared to normal prisons. In California, a legislative commission concluded that it costs the state an *extra* $90,000 for each death row inmate per year compared to the costs of the same inmate housed in general population. With over 670 inmates on death row, that amounts to an additional yearly cost of $60 million solely attributable to the death penalty.

A Better Choice: Life Without Parole

It is important to note that all of these expenses are incurred in the many death penalty cases that never result in an execution. Sentences or convictions can be reversed, defendants may die of natural causes or suicide, governors occasionally grant clemency, and entire statutes can be overturned by the courts. This often means that a life sentence is the end result, but only after a very expensive death penalty process. According to one comprehensive study, 68% of death penalty cases are reversed at some point in the appeals process. When these cases are retried without the defect that led to the reversal, 82% result in a sentence of life or less.

This is an extremely wasteful process. The most prevalent cause for reversal on appeal is the inadequacy of the trial counsel. Frequently, this is the result of courts trying to cut costs by short-changing due process. States that appoint inexperienced lawyers at low fees, or which deny the experts and resources necessary for thorough representation, may end up paying for two trials, with the second one resulting in a life sentence. In most cases a life sentence could have been obtained at the outset of the case for a fraction of the cost. It is the *pursuit* of the death penalty that is so expensive. . . .

Justice can be achieved far more reliably and equitably without the death penalty.

It is doubtful in today's economic climate that any legislature would introduce the death penalty if faced with the reality that each execution would cost taxpayers $25 million, or that the state might spend more than $100 million over several years and produce few or no executions. Surely there are more pressing needs deserving funding, such as retaining police officers, rebuilding roads and bridges, creating jobs, providing health care for children, and keeping libraries open. Yet that is precisely the dilemma that many states with the death penalty now face.

Referring to the costs of the death penalty often evokes a response that money is irrelevant when it comes to justice and a safer society. But the death penalty is not essential to those goals, as the 15 states in the U.S. and the growing majority of countries in the world without the death penalty have demonstrated. Even states with the death penalty rarely use it. Justice can be achieved far more reliably and equitably without the death penalty. There are more efficient ways of making society safer.

The economic crisis that began in 2008 continues, and its impact on states will be felt for years to come. There is no reason the death penalty should be immune from reconsideration, along with other wasteful, expensive programs that no longer make sense. The promised benefits from the death penalty have not materialized. Deterrence is not credible; vengeance in the name of a few victims in a handful of states is both divisive and debilitating. If more states choose to end the death penalty, it will hardly be missed, and the economic savings will be significant. The positive programs that can be funded once this economic burden is lifted will be readily apparent. Such an approach would be smart on crime.

15

Women Are More Often
Spared the Death Penalty

Gabrielle Banks

Gabrielle Banks is a contributing writer for the Pittsburgh Post-Gazette *newspaper.*

Women are less apt to commit violent crimes than men, but when they do, they are given disproportionately fewer death sentences. Anecdotal evidence has shown that this partiality may be due to a woman's physical appearance; women are usually smaller, more demur and seemingly vulnerable, and are more able than men to cry and play-act for jurors' sympathy. Also, in most cases female defendants kill family members rather than strangers, leading jurors to believe mental illness or emotional trauma prompted the crime instead of cold-blooded, premeditated brutality. It should be made clear that women have been executed in the state system over the years—the astoundingly low number of executions is a result of federal executions compared to state executions.

Very few women get condemned to death in America.

Mercer County [Ohio] widow Donna Moonda could join these lean ranks this week [July 2007] if a federal jury gives her the maximum penalty for hiring her boyfriend to kill her husband along the Ohio Turnpike.

If that happens and she exhausts her appeals, Mrs. Moonda could be the first woman in 50 years to be executed on a federal conviction and only the second woman since Ethel Rosenberg to go to the death chamber for a federal crime.

Historical records indicate the only other woman executed for a federal offense was Mary Surratt, who was hanged for conspiring to kill Abraham Lincoln.

Characteristics of Female Offenders

Women who are executed differ from their male counterparts both in the nature of their crimes and in the way they are treated in the criminal justice system. They tend to be older when they commit their crimes than the men who are executed. Their victims are more likely to be family members than strangers. In some cases, prosecutors don't consider the death penalty for a woman when they might seek it for a man committing the same crime. Also, anecdotal evidence suggests women have a better shot at beating a death sentence or avoiding execution if they're good-looking.

Women are less apt to commit violent crimes, but they also end up with disproportionately fewer death sentences, said Elizabeth Rapaport, a law professor at University of New Mexico who studies women and the death penalty.

Women can be tried for capital convictions when there are aggravating factors, for example, multiple victims or if the defendant plotted a murder.

Juries and judges can be more forgiving and governors are sometimes more prone to grant women clemency after conviction, said Victor L. Streib, an Ohio Northern University law professor who has studied the outcomes for female prisoners sentenced to death since 1632.

A classic example of this judicial disparity is the case of Susan Smith, a white woman from South Carolina who intentionally rolled her Mazda into a lake in 1994, drowning her two sleeping sons who were buckled into car seats. She initially told police that a black man carjacked the vehicle and abducted the boys. She made pleas on television for help.

When her story fell apart, the local district attorney, who was up for re-election, thought it would be a slam dunk conviction, but her trial lawyers presented evidence of abuse and depression and the jury voted for a life sentence. Susan Smith will be eligible for parole in 17 years at the age of 53.

The common attributes among female offenders are tough to nail down. The majority of women on death row are mothers. Most kill victims of their same race. Donna Moonda would be typical in the sense that about half the women who get the death penalty for murdering a husband or boyfriend hired the assassin, which is atypical for male offenders.

"Women are less likely to do the dirty work," Mr. Streib said. He also said it would be unusual for a woman who plotted the murder to get a lighter sentence than the triggerman, but other scholars said it would not be unprecedented.

This bodes well for Mrs. Moonda, 48, whose former boyfriend helped prosecutors secure a conviction by testifying that he shot Dr. Gulam Moonda on the side of the road according to her plan. For his cooperation, the 26-year-old drug dealer got a 17 1/2-year sentence. While the men imprisoned for conspiring with Mary Surratt and Ethel Rosenberg were hanged and electrocuted, Damian Bradford could be a free man by the age of 40.

Evidence of Bias

In the 1972 *Furman v. Georgia* ruling that briefly suspended the death penalty, the Supreme Court noted a consistent racial disparity in the execution of blacks and whites for the same crimes.

Justice Thurgood Marshall also noted gender bias in application of the law: "There is also overwhelming evidence that the death penalty is employed against men and not women. Only 32 women have been executed since 1930, while 3,827 men have met a similar fate. It is difficult to understand why women have received such favored treatment since the purposes allegedly served by capital punishment seemingly are equally applicable to both sexes."

The earliest documented capital convictions of women were in colonial New England and Maryland where a couple dozen women in their teens and early 20s were hanged or drowned for witchcraft. A Massachusetts woman was sent to the gallows in 1643 for committing adultery.

Between 1712 and 1741, New York and Louisiana hanged several female slaves for rising up against slaveowners. In some cases female slaves were executed because their masters' children took ill and died in their care.

In the past three decades, women have accounted for 1 percent of executions. While the percentage of condemned women hasn't risen significantly since the early 20th century, the legal reasoning for handing down life sentences has become more covert.

"In the 1940s and '50s, judges would say on the record, 'I'm giving you life because you're a mother.' Now they just think that, but don't say why they're being more lenient,'" said Mr. Streib, the legal historian at Ohio Northern. He said the discrepancies "have nothing to do with law, it's about mercy and playing on the emotions of the jury."

He suggested that women get life in prison based on the same gut-level reasoning that dictated women and children had first dibs on the lifeboats when the Titanic started sinking.

A woman's physical appearance appears to have some impact on legal strategies and outcomes in death penalty cases.

Governors usually have the final call on impending executions, a task that bears heavily on some. While he was governor of Texas, George W. Bush had to decide the fate of Karla Faye Tucker, a process he described in his autobiography, *A Charge to Keep*, as the "longest 20 minutes of my tenure as governor" and "one of the hardest things I have ever done."

President Bush's friend, the conservative televangelist Pat Robertson, pleaded for clemency and the then-governor's own daughter appealed for mercy for Karla Faye at the dinner table. In the two years prior, Mr. Bush had approved nearly 60 executions. A clue to the governor's trepidation about killing Karla Faye Tucker lies in this appraisal from the book: "Hers was a pleasant face, a smiling face, a sympathetic face. At five-three and 120 pounds, with wavy brown hair and large expressive eyes, Karla Faye Tucker did not fit the public image of a typical death-row inmate. She seemed contrite and sincere. She had found Jesus and salvation."

The former prostitute had helped slay two people with a pickax while high on drugs.

Women are able to play-act and cry on cue.

Despite a high execution rate, Texas had not executed a woman since 1863, but the board of pardons tied his hands, he wrote, and he let the Huntsville prison officials carry out their task.

Mr. Streib said Mr. Bush's trepidation in this instance is a factor defense lawyers are fully aware of: "I know when I consult on these cases we talk about making [female defendants] look demure, vulnerable, not in control and not sexy so the jury might find some sympathy for them." The ideal look, he said, is the "Trisha Nixon type with downcast eyes and white gloves."

There's also some coaching that goes into defending a woman in a capital case. "It's terribly sexist but women are able to play-act and cry on cue. More males have a difficult time showing their emotions or the appearance of remorse," he said.

To combat this type of sentimental appeal, prosecutors make an effort to "dehumanize and defeminize" women on death row, he said.

Before Judy Buenano's death, prosecutors took pains to ensure that the only image the public saw of the 54-year-old was her mug shot, Mr. Streib said. One month after Karla Faye Tucker's hotly debated execution, Florida's infamous "Black Widow" was electrocuted for killing her husband and stealing a car with far less public outcry.

Coverage of the bedraggled looking Aileen Wuornos, played by Charlize Theron in the 2003 film *Monster*, focused on how the former prostitute was a rare exception as a female serial killer. In the buildup to her Florida execution in 2002, the public knew she was unrepentant for slaying seven men, but reporters gave less airtime to what defense lawyers argued were severe mental health issues.

Greater Leniency with Domestic Homicides

There are several readily apparent explanations for why so few women get the death penalty. Women who kill their children are more likely to win an insanity defense, because society cannot fathom how a mother could do that to her child. Andrea Yates appealed her life sentence for drowning her five children and after she won an appeal, a second jury found her not guilty by reason of insanity.

Violence that stems from domestic abuse is assessed differently by society, so legal outcomes for violent women are often different, said Ms. Rapaport, the death penalty scholar at the University of New Mexico.

Society doesn't view as seriously the type of domestic homicides women generally commit.

Former Ohio Gov. Richard F. Celeste granted clemency to 25 female inmates after reviewing the work of Ohio State University sociologists who interviewed all female inmates at the state penitentiary at Marysville. The study found many women convicted of killing a husband or boyfriend suffered from "battered women's syndrome," but the existing law prevented them from introducing this evidence at trial.

The governor then commuted the death sentences of all four women and four of 97 men on death row in his last days in office, drawing criticism from victims' rights groups.

Most homicide convictions for women are not capital convictions because society doesn't view as seriously the type of domestic homicides women generally commit in the heat of passion as it does cold-blooded killings or slayings that occur in the course of a robbery or rape, Ms. Rapaport said.

"You can terrorize your family, but people still pity you because of your emotional trauma," she said. Terrorizing a stranger is something jurors can picture and fear, but they often can't imagine their families would harm them.

Editor's Note: *On September 21, 2007, a federal jury sentenced Donna Moonda to life in prison for plotting and helping in the May 13, 2005, murder of her husband. Moonda's boyfriend followed her family on a road trip, approached her husband's car when stopped along the Ohio Turnpike, and pretended to rob the family so that he could shoot and kill Dr. Gulam Moonda. Prosecutors had sought the death penalty.*

Organizations to Contact

The editors have compiled the following list of organizations concerned with the issues debated in this book. The descriptions are derived from materials provided by the organizations. All have publications or information available for interested readers. The list was compiled on the date of publication of the present volume; the information provided here may change. Readers need to remember that many organizations take several weeks or longer to respond to inquiries.

American Civil Liberties Union (ACLU)
125 Broad St., 18th Fl., New York, NY   10004
(212) 549-2500 • fax: (212) 549-2646
e-mail: aclu@aclu.org
website: www.aclu.org

The ACLU believes that capital punishment violates the Constitution's ban on cruel and unusual punishment as well as the requirements of due process and equal protection under the law. Its Capital Punishment Project is dedicated to abolishing the death penalty. The ACLU maintains the "Blog of Rights" and publishes numerous books and pamphlets, including *The Case against the Death Penalty*.

Amnesty International USA (AI)
5 Penn Plaza, New York, NY   10001
(212) 807-8400 • fax: (212) 627-1451
e-mail: aimember@aiusa.org
website: www.amnestyusa.org

Amnesty International USA's Death Penalty Abolition Campaign seeks the abolishment of the death penalty worldwide. Its most recent activities have been aimed at decreasing the use of the death penalty internationally, including in the United States, and increasing the number of countries that have removed the death penalty as an option for punishment. It also serves as advocate in individual clemency cases. Amnesty International USA publishes news, fact sheets, and reports, including *The Death Penalty Resource Guide* and *Amnesty International Debates the Death Penalty.*

Campaign to End the Death Penalty (CEDP)

PO Box 25730, Chicago, IL 60625
(773) 955-4841 • fax: (773) 955-4842
website: www.nodeathpenalty.org

The CEDP is a national grassroots organization dedicated to the abolition of capital punishment in the United States. Its website contains local contact information, regular updates on death-row cases, and fact sheets about capital punishment in the United States. The CEDP regularly publishes a newsletter, *The New Abolitionist.*

Catholics Against Capital Punishment (CACP)

PO Box 5706, Bethesda, MD 20824-5706
fax: (301) 654-0925
e-mail: ellen.frank@verizon.net
website: www.cacp.org

Founded in 1992 to promote the Catholic Church's teachings about capital punishment, Catholics Against Capital Punishment is a national organization that works to stop the death penalty in the United States. The organization's newsletter, *CACP News Notes* is published four to six times a year.

Criminal Justice Legal Foundation (CJLF)

PO Box 1199, Sacramento, CA 95812
(916) 446-0345
website: www.cjlf.org

The Criminal Justice Legal Foundation was established in 1982 as a nonprofit, public interest law organization dedicated to restoring a balance between the rights of crime victims and the accused. The CJLF sponsors the blog "Crime & Consequences," and its website offers links to various transcripts, articles, and working papers, including "The Death Penalty and Plea Bargaining to Life Sentences."

Death Penalty Information Center (DPIC)
1015 18th St. NW, #704, Washington, DC   20036
(202) 289-2275 • fax: (202) 289-7336
website: www.deathpenaltyinfo.org

DPIC opposes the death penalty because it believes that capital punishment is discriminatory, costly to taxpayers, and may result in innocent persons being put to death. Its website publishes public opinion reports, testimony, news articles, and reports about public views on the death penalty, including "Smart on Crime: Reconsidering the Death Penalty in a Time of Economic Crisis" and "A Crisis of Confidence: Americans' Doubts About the Death Penalty."

Equal Justice Initiative (EJI)
122 Commerce St., Montgomery, AL   36104
(334) 269-1803 • fax: (334) 269-1806
e-mail: contact_us@eji.org
website: www.eji.org

A nonprofit organization, the Equal Justice Initiative provides legal representation to indigent defendants and prisoners who have been denied fair and just treatment in the legal system. EJI also prepares reports, newsletters, and manuals to assist advocates and policymakers in reforming the criminal justice system. Its website offers videos, news articles, and reports, including "Cruel and Unusual: Sentencing 13- and 14-Year-Old Children to Die in Prison."

Innocence Project
100 Fifth Ave., 3rd Fl., New York, NY   10011
(212) 364-5340
e-mail: info@innocenceproject.org
website: www.innocenceproject.org

The Innocence Project is dedicated to exonerating wrongfully convicted people through DNA testing and reforming the criminal justice system to prevent future injustice. As of July 2008, it has assisted in the exoneration of 218 people in the United States, each of whom served an average of twelve years in prison, including sixteen who served time on death row. The Innocence Project publishes the "Innocence Blog," monthly e-newsletters, fact sheets, and reports, including *Lineups: Why Witnesses Make Mistakes and How to Reduce the Chance of a Misidentification.*

Justice Fellowship (JF)

44180 Riverside Parkway, Lansdowne, VA   20176
(877) 478-0100
e-mail: justicefellowship@pfm.org
website: www.justicefellowship.org

This Christian organization bases its work for reform of the justice system on the concept of victim-offender reconciliation. It does not take a position on the death penalty. On its website, JF publishes true stories of restoration as well as the "Justice eReport" and other commentary and reports, including *Capital Punishment: A Call to Dialogue* and *Monitoring Death Sentencing Decisions: The Challenges and Barriers to Equity.*

Justice for All (JFA)

PO Box 55159, Houston, TX   77255
(713) 935-9300 • fax: (713) 935-9301
e-mail: info@jfa.net
website: www.jfa.net

Justice for All is an all-volunteer, nonprofit criminal justice reform organization that supports the death penalty. Its activities include publishing the monthly newsletter *The Voice of Justice* and circulating online petitions to keep violent offenders from being paroled early.

Lincoln Institute for Research and Education

PO Box 254, Great Falls, VA 22066
(703) 759-4278 • fax: (703) 759-4597
e-mail: contactus@lincolnreview.com
website: www.lincolnreview.com

The institute is a conservative think tank that studies public policy issues affecting the lives of black Americans, including the issue of the death penalty, which it favors. It publishes commentary, Amicus Briefs, and the *Lincoln Letter Review.*

National Coalition to Abolish the Death Penalty (NCADP)

1705 DeSales Street, NW, Fifth Fl., Washington, DC 20036
(202) 331-4090
website: www.ncadp.org

The National Coalition to Abolish the Death Penalty is a collection of more than 100 groups working together to stop executions in the United States and throughout the world. The organization compiles statistics on the death penalty. To further its goal, the coalition publishes blogs, information packets, pamphlets, research materials, and the quarterly newsletter *LifeLines.*

National Criminal Justice Reference Service (NCJRS)

PO Box 6000, Rockville, MD 20849-6000
(301) 519-5500 • fax: (301) 519-5212
website: www.ncjrs.gov

Established in 1972, the National Criminal Justice Reference Service is a federally funded resource offering justice information to support research, policy, and program development worldwide. NCJRS hosts one of the largest criminal and juvenile justice libraries and databases in the world. Among its many publications are the bi-weekly electronic newsletter *JUSTINFO* and the report *Justice Delayed? Time Consumption in Capital Appeals: A Multistate Study.*

United States Department of Justice (DOJ)

950 Pennsylvania Avenue, NW, Washington, DC   20530-0001
(202) 514-2000
e-mail: AskDOJ@usdoj.gov
website: www.usdoj.gov

The mission of the Department of Justice is to enforce U.S. law, provide federal leadership in preventing and controlling crime, seek just punishment for those guilty of unlawful behavior, and ensure fair and impartial administration of justice for all Americans. Its website publishes press releases, *The Justice Blog*, and various reports, including *Capital Punishment Statistical Tables*.

Bibliography

Books

Howard W. Allen
and Jerome M.
Clubb

*Race, Class, and the Death Penalty:
Capital Punishment in American
History.* Albany, NY: State University
of New York Press, 2009.

Robert Baldwin

*Life and Death Matters: Seeking the
Truth About Capital Punishment.*
Montgomery, AL: New South Books,
2009.

Frank R.
Baumgartner

*The Decline of the Death Penalty and
the Discovery of Innocence.*
Cambridge, MA: Cambridge
University Press, 2008.

Thomas Cahill

*A Saint on Death Row: The Story of
Dominique Green.* New York:
Doubleday, 2009.

Scott
Christianson

*The Last Gas: The Rise and Fall of the
American Gas Chamber.* Berkeley, CA:
University of California Press, 2010.

David R. Dow

The Autobiography of an Execution.
New York: Twelve, 2010.

Robert K. Elder

Last Words of the Executed. Chicago:
University of Chicago Press, 2010.

Rudolph Joseph
Gerber and John
M. Johnson

*The Top Ten Death Penalty Myths:
The Politics of Crime Control.*
Westport, CT: Praeger Publishers,
2007.

John Grisham   *The Innocent Man: Murder and Injustice in a Small Town.* New York: Dell, 2007.

Dale Jacquette *Dialogues on the Ethics of Capital Punishment.* Lanham, MD: Rowman and Littlefield, 2009.

Andrea D. Lyon *Angel of Death Row: My Life as a Death Penalty Defense Lawyer.* New York: Kaplan Publishing, 2010.

David M. Oshinsky *Capital Punishment on Trial: Furman v. Georgia and the Death Penalty in Modern America.* Lawrence, KS: University Press of Kansas, 2010.

Raymond Paternoster, Robert Brame, and Sarah Bacon *The Death Penalty: America's Experience with Capital Punishment.* New York: Oxford University Press, 2007.

Helen Prejean *The Death of Innocence: An Eyewitness Account of Wrongful Executions.* New York: Vintage, 2006.

Austin Sarat *The Road to Abolition?: The Future of Capital Punishment in the United States.* New York University Press, 2009.

Billy Wayne Sinclair and Jodie Sinclair *Capital Punishment: An Indictment by a Death-Row Survivor.* New York: Arcade, 2009.

Victor Streib *The Fairer Death: Executing Women in Ohio.* Athens, OH: Ohio University Press, 2006.

Scott E. Sundby   *A Life and Death Decision: A Jury
                      Weighs the Death Penalty.* New York:
                      Palgrave Macmillan, 2007.

Franklin E.   *Executions, Deterrence and Homicide:
Zimring   A Tale of Two Cities.* Berkeley, CA:
                      University of California Press, 2009.

Periodicals and Internet Sources

Mike Adams   "Our States' Right to Kill the Rapist,"
                      Townhall.com, June 2, 2008.

Joan   "Those Most Affected Help Analysts
Arehart-Treichel   Mull Death Penalty," *Psychiatric
                      News*, Vol. 43, No. 5, March 7, 2008.

Associated Press   "Court Weighs Death for Child
                      Rapists: Is Execution Appropriate or
                      Cruel and Unusual Punishment?"
                      April 16, 2008.

Ed Barnes   "Just or Not, Cost of Death Penalty
                      Is a Killer for State Budgets,"
                      FOXNews.com, March 27, 2010.

Douglas A.   "Engaging Capital Emotions,"
Berman and   *Northwestern University Law Review*,
Stephanos Bibas   Vol. 103, 2008.

Lee Black and   "Lethal Injection and Physicians:
Robert M. Sade   State Law vs. Medical Ethics," *Journal
                      of the American Medical Association*,
                      Vol. 298, No. 23-2779, December 19,
                      2007.

Sabrina Bogan   "The Death Penalty and the Wrongly Convicted," *Associated Content*, June 4, 2009.

Jack Broom   "Death Penalty Rare for Women," *Seattle Times*, December 30, 2007.

Matthew Continetti   "An Indecent Decision: Justice Kennedy's Atrocious Child Rape Ruling," *The Weekly Standard*, Vol. 013, Issue 41, July 7, 2008.

Mark H. Creech   "A Christian Response to Death Penalty Issues," *Intellectual Conservative*, January 30, 2007.

Mary C. Curtis   "Death Row Inmates Get Reprieve with Racial Justice Act," PoliticsDaily.com, August 20, 2009.

Jennifer Dobner   "Firing Squad Executes Utah Killer," *Associated Press*, June 19, 2010.

John Donohue and Justin Wolfers   "The Death Penalty: No Evidence of Deterrence," *Economists' Voice*, April 2006.

Erika Encinas   "Death Penalty in U.S. Is Deterrent for Potential Crimes," *Collegiate Times*, April 30, 2009.

Marc Fisher   "After Aunt's Murder, Deligate Views Death as Fair Penalty," *Washington Post*, March 6, 2009.

Laura Fitzpatrick   "The Death Penalty: Racist, Classist and Unfair," *Time*, February 23, 2010.

Marvis Hackett-Walker	"A Matter of Rehabilitation," *American Chronicle*, July 2, 2008.
Harold Hall	"A Sentence Too Close to Death: Wrongly Convicted, I Am Proof that the State Should Reconsider Execution," *Los Angeles Times*, March 27, 2008.
Jennie Hanba	"Controversies Regarding the Death Penalty in the United States," *Associated Content*, September 9, 2009.
Earl Ofari Hutchinson	"Gender Bias: Linda Carty's Last Hope on Death Row," *New America Media*, March 3, 2010.
Joseph Klein	"The Supreme Court at Work: The Constitution vs. World Opinion," FrontPageMag.com, April 22, 2008.
Adam Liptak	"Does Death Penalty Save Lives? A New Debate," *New York Times*, November 18, 2007.
David Masci and Jesse Merriam	"An Impassioned Debate: An Overview of the Death Penalty in America," *Pew Forum*, December 19, 2007.
Scott Michels	"The Death Penalty and the 'Plague of Racism,'" TheCrimeReport.org, November 2, 2009.
Jonathan Morris	"The Death Penalty Goes to Court," FoxNews.com, March 28, 2008.

David B. Muhlhausen	"The Death Penalty Deters Crime and Saves Lives," The Heritage Foundation, www.heritage.org, August 28, 2007.
Susan Olp	"Wrongly Convicted Man Speaks Against Death Penalty," *Billings Gazette*, January 30, 2010.
Martin O'Malley	"Why I Oppose the Death Penalty," *Washington Post*, February 21, 2007.
Kevin B. O'Reilly	"Doctor Quits Prison Job over Execution," *American Medical News*, February 9, 2009.
Pew Research Center	"Lethal Injection on Trial: An Analysis of the Arguments Before the Supreme Court in Baze v. Rees," PewForum.org, December 19, 2007.
Gabriella Porrino	"Death to the Death Penalty," *Columbia Spectator*, November 29, 2009.
Bert Roughton III	"Rethinking the Death Penalty," LikeTheDew.com, June 25, 2009.
Debra J. Saunders	"Keep Life Without Parole, Life After Death," Townhall.com, August 1, 2009.
Margo Schulter	"Martin Luther King Day: Retribution and Rehabilitation," DeathPenalty.org, January 22, 2009.
Robert Schwartz	"The Effect of Baze v. Rees on Death Penalty Reform," CivilRights.org, April 18, 2008.

Erin Sheley "The Supreme Penalty: Arguing About the Death Penalty Yet Again," *The Weekly Standard*, Vol. 013, Issue 28, March 31, 2008.

Cassy Stubbs "The Death Penalty Deterrence Myth: No Solid Evidence That Killing Stops the Killing," *The Huffington Post*, June 18, 2007, www.huffington post.com.

Cass R. Sunstein and Justin Wolfers "A Death Penalty Puzzle: The Murky Evidence for and Against Deterrence," *Washington Post*, June 30, 2008.

Andrew Tallman "Why Would Anyone Support Capital Punishment?" Crosswalk.com, February 4, 2008.

Robert Tanner "Studies Say Death Penalty Deters Crime," *Associated Press*, June 11, 2007.

Cal Thomas "A Matter of Life and Death," JewishWorldReview.com, April 22, 2008.

John Wilkens "Hollow Promise?" *San Diego Union Tribune*, April 25, 2010.

Byron Williams "Troy Davis Case Shows Why Death Penalty Must Be Eliminated," *The Huffington Post*, October 30, 2008, www.huffingtonpost.com.

Carol J. Williams "Death Row Foes Now Fight the Cost of Executions," *Los Angeles Times*, June 30, 2009.

Jeanne Woodford "Death Row Realism: Do Executions Make Us Safer? San Quentin's Former Warden Says No," *Los Angeles Times*, October 2, 2008.

Russ Wung   "Forensic Advances Make Capital Punishment Safer, More Just," *The Daily*, November 10, 2009.

Index

N

New York, New York, 33
Nondoctors, physicians as, 70–72, 77–78
Nonhomicide cases, 43
North Carolina
    Medical Board, 58, 76
    Racial Justice Act, 57–60, 61–64

P

Payne v. Tennessee, 14
Pepperdine University study, 31–32
Perdue, Beverly, 61, 62
Peremptory challenges, 13–14, 21
Physicians
    dual loyalty, 66–67
    Hippocratic oath, 67–70
    hypocrisy and "do no harm," 73–79
    as Nondoctors, 70–72, 77–78
    North Carolina Medical Board, 58
Police, 94–95
Political crimes, 84–85
Political dissent, 87
Poor persons, 27
Proportionality in child rape cases, 41–43, 46, 49
Prosecutors, 8
Public opinion, 7–8
Public trust, 68–70
Punishment
    bifurcated standards of proof in capital cases, 91–92
    eye for an eye justice, 24–25
    life imprisonment *vs.* capital punishment, 25–26

R

Racial discrimination, 14–15, 27, 57–60, 61–64
Racial Justice Act (North Carolina), 57–60, 61–64
Reasonable doubt *vs.* beyond a lingering doubt, 91–92
Recidivism, 28–29
Rehabilitation, 33
Reporting, 48
Retribution
    child rape cases, 46–48
    eye for an eye justice, 23–24, 32, 90
    as primary rationale, 11–13
    punishment without pain, 19–20
    vengeance disguised as, 85–86
Revenge, 26–27, 85–86
Reversals, 98–99
Robertson, Pat, 106
Rosenberg, Ethel, 103
Ryan, George, 8–9

S

Scalia, Antonin Gregory, 16–22
Self defense, 82
Sentencing
    aggravating circumstances, 44–45, 52–53
    discretion, 52
    standard of proof, 91–92
Smith, Richard D., 62–63
Smith, Susan, 103–104
Standard of proof, 91–92
State legislatures, 16–17, 19, 21–22
Statistics
    analysis, 36–37
    discrimination, 62–64